Disneyland's Back Door

Disneyland's Back Door

& OTHER GREAT STORIES

James D'Arcy Standish

www.BrownRoadBooks.com

Ordering Information:
Quantity sales: Special discounts are available on quantity purchases by bookstores, wholesalers, schools, churches, corporations, associations, and others. For details, contact the publisher at the web address above.

Oral performance of the stories: The author grants permission to orally read or retell the stories in this book in churches, schools and any worship related activity provided that at every oral performance, the following is stated: "This story comes from a book called *Disneyland's Back Door*, written by James Standish and available from Brown Road Books." If you're feeling particularly generous, you might even say "a *marvelous* book by James Standish *that every one of you really should get!*"

Each story in this book is based on a real event, but is not a literal retelling of that event. Rather, names have been changed, important details amended, characters augmented or changed and, in some stories, characters added or removed. Events, locales and conversations are not as they literally occurred. In order to maintain anonymity, names of most individuals have been changed, as have the names of some places, some identifying characteristics and details such as physical properties, occupations and places of residence. The characters and events within the book are not factual records of any person, living or deceased.

Printed in the United States of America

Publisher's Cataloging-in-Publication data
Standish, James.
Disneyland's Back Door/James Standish
p. cm.
ISBN-13: 9781539893622
ISBN-10: 1539893626
Library of Congress Control Number: 2016918841
CreateSpace Independent Publishing Platform
North Charleston, South Carolina

1. The main category of the book —Teen. 2. Adventure. 3. Christian. 4. Travel.
5. Children. 6. History.
HF0000.A0 A00 2010
299.000 00–dc22 2010999999

First Edition

14 13 12 11 10 / 10 9 8 7 6 5 4 3 2 1

Dedicated to Three Beautiful Women
Dr. Leisa Morton-Standish, Shea Isobel Standish &
Skye D'Arcy Standish

Sincere thanks to those who assisted and encouraged me with this project, particularly the rock of my life, Dr. Leisa Morton-Standish, good friends Pr. Gary and Bettina Krause, and all the kids who heard these stories and said, "You should write a book!"

Table of Contents

What They're Saying About "Disneyland's Back Door"

"Literally laugh out loud and fall down and can't recover for a while funny! My daughter was in stitches, as was I. Very clever, creative and powerfully faith-affirming story telling." Nicholas Miller, professor and father of three, Andrews University, Michigan, USA.

"This book needs to come with a warning... DON'T LET ADULTS GET THEIR HANDS ON IT FIRST. I know that this is a children's book, but the kids will just have to wait till the adults have finished reading, laughing, crying and reflecting! Great stories for kids of all ages." Ian Sweeney, church leader, ENGLAND.

"James' stories are always engaging and thought provoking. They are a big favorite at our house!" Jennifer Price, lawyer, & Craig Price, executive, parents of six children, Sydney, AUSTRALIA.

"It's refreshing to read a Christian children's book that doesn't condescend to kids and gets what interests them. It has history, travel, theology, all wrapped within adventure and humor. We love it almost as much as our daughter does!" Gary Krause, church leader, & Bettina Krause, lawyer, Maryland, USA.

"James is a uniquely talented and accomplished storyteller with a knack for vivid, hilariously funny and inspiring stories. He creates a wonderful visual of characters and everyday situations, and the stories, through little glimpses of his life, make you reflect on your own life and some of the bigger issues and dilemmas facing us all, while being entertained and inspired in the process." Vidar Keyn, business advisor and father of two, Oslo, NORWAY.

"James' stories are joyful, fun, full of amazing life experiences from all over the world, and they are deeply spiritual. Our students love them - as do our teachers!" Judie Rosa, school vice principal and mother of three, Maryland, USA.

"James' writing is comical, pointed as well as spiritually relevant for our children. Love his material!" Terry Johnson, church leader, Perth, AUSTRALIA.

"James is a master writer of contemporary Christian children stories. A great read for both parent and child." JC Crissey, businessman and father of two, ENGLAND.

"The first story in the book is told with great humor through the eyes of a boy 'launched' in a new country and having his first hilarious 'donut' experience via his peculiar roommate. This short story grabs the reader until the end and comes with a profound lesson." Dominique Ledra, mother of two, Cairns, FRANCE.

"James' fun and fascinating narrative world creates the ideal place where he weaves deep spiritual truths with an unforgettable bang. And, wonderfully, neither mind nor heart (or funny bone) are ever left behind." Anthony MacPherson, theologian and father of two, Suva, FIJI.

"James' stories are thought provoking and great *kopfkino* as we say in German, which means cinema in the head. And good cinema always touches my heart. I want this book for my grandchildren!" Herbert Bodenmann, media spokesman, Basel, SWITZERLAND.

"James is a master story teller. The students and I love his stories." Bob Uhrig, school chaplain, Maryland, USA

About this Book

There's really only two kinds of books: books worth reading. And those that aren't. But how do you tell them apart? Easy. Flip them open in the middle and start to read. If the story grabs you, it's a keeper. If you find your eyes closing, your body slumping and drool seeping out the side of your mouth? Whatever you do, put that book back before it does any more damage!

So which kind of book is this book?

Flip it open and find out! You'll soon be crawling through dark, cramped tunnels far beneath a forgotten fort in search of answers. You'll stand with the other kids in the dorm cheering as Charlie faces down the chili challenge - or does he? You'll stare into the heaving molten lava of an exploding volcano on a far, far away tropical island. You'll walk the halls of the most beautiful house in the world, with its elegant, but shady, owner. All of that, and an awful lot more.

So, don't waste your time reading this. Open up the book and get lost in the adventure!

Danny & the Mystery Donuts

This story is all about donuts. Beautiful, sweet, golden brown donuts melting in your mouth just when you could not be hungrier for a little snack. I can smell them now - the rich dark chocolate icing, the crispy brown shell on the outside, and creamy smooth caramel filling waiting to ooze out with the first bite.

I'd never thought much about donuts until I arrived at a completely new boarding school, in a completely new town, in a completely new country. At least they were all completely new to me!

The town, located in the middle of Michigan, was tiny, but the boarding school was the largest school I'd ever attended. I felt lost among all the kids.

To be honest, I didn't know very much about Michigan before I arrived. I'd never been there. I didn't know anyone at all who lived there. And I didn't know anything about life there.

Just as well, as if I had known, I never would have gone! No way. No how.

Why?

Because I grew up in hot places. There is literally no winter in Southeast Asia where I was raised in my missionary family. It never even gets cool. And as for snow? That's just something you might see on TV.

It never occurred to me just how cold Michigan would be – and for how long. I didn't know it was possible to be that cold!

But I'm glad I didn't know, because that year in Michigan was just so, so wonderful.

And the magic of the year all started with a mysterious donut.

How? You'll see soon enough…

$$\sim$$

First you need to know that the day I arrived in Michigan was one of the worst days of my life.

I flew into the big city of Detroit - which is a very intimidating place to be a kid all alone. And I was alone for a long time, because no one from the school showed up to meet me! I didn't know anyone in Michigan so there wasn't even anyone I could call. I just stood with my bags hoping that sooner or later someone from the school would show up.

I waited and I waited and I waited.

Almost two hours after I landed, someone finally showed up. Phew, that was a huge relief! Maybe things would get better from there?

But when I arrived at the high school, I realized my trouble was just starting. I saw kids having fun together. I saw friends running up to each other after the long summer vacation - excited to be back together again. I saw them playing games I'd never seen before. And right then I realized – I don't know any of them. Not one guy or one girl. All their friendships were so deep and strong after years of knowing each other. Why would any of them want to be friends with me - the new kid?

All my friends? They were almost 9,000 miles away at my old school in Singapore. And as for my parents? They were in Thailand. What a huge mistake to come to a new school for my senior year! I never felt more lonely in all my life.

But something changed all of that, and that something was a boy named Danny.

Danny had very pale skin. Lots and lots of freckles. A smallish nose turned up a little at the end. The most mischievous smile you've ever seen, on his round face. But none of that was what stood out the most.

For that, you had to look up. You see, he had the frizziest ginger hair you've ever seen. And it stood up on the top of his head like a little forest. It stood so high, that when he shook his head, his hair kind of wobbled all on its own.

Danny was the kind of boy who found curious people interesting. Or was it that he found interesting people curious? Either way, as soon as he heard I was an Australian kid who had flown in from Singapore, well that was fascinating to him.

Danny wanted to know all about the Malaysian tropical island where I grew up. He wanted to know about Australia, where my family was from originally. He was interested in our house in Thailand and my old boarding school in Singapore. Danny wanted to know about all the places I'd visited and all the unusual things I'd seen.

But most of all, Danny wanted to know how on earth I had ended up in Michigan for my last year of high school. "Who goes to a new school for their last year?" he asked. "And why?" I didn't really want to say! But Danny was very persistent, and you just really couldn't say no to him. So I told him and made him promise to keep it a secret as it was very embarrassing. I suppose I will tell you too - a little later...

∽

One thing about boarding school is that once the front doors are closed at night, you can't leave. And that's very bad news if your tummy starts to rumble. Sometimes you're studying hard, and it's late, and you didn't eat much supper, and, oooh, you'd give almost anything for a little snack! But you can't get one because those big old doors are shut and you'll be in just so much trouble if you go out them.

And that's where Danny came in. You see Danny had a business selling donuts to hungry classmates late at night.

But there was a problem. I didn't have any money. My parents were missionaries. I mean, we were really poor! There was no way I had money to spend on crispy, sweet, perfectly browned donuts covered in chocolate icing - no matter how good they smelled after a tough evening of study!

As I was walking by Danny's dorm room one night, the wonderful smell of donuts was wafting out his open door and all the boys were in there buying donuts. Danny yelled out to me as I walked by, "Hey, James, ya wanna donut?"

Of course I wanted a donut! But I had to say, "Sorry, Danny, I don't have any cash." To be honest, I felt a little humiliated. I mean, who doesn't have a buck for a donut? But here comes the really surprising bit. He laughed and said, "Ah, you can just have one!" And he handed me a delicious donut.

Ohh, it was so, so good! I don't think I've ever eaten a sweeter, crispier, softer more tasty donut in all my life. It just melted in my mouth. I was in a state of total donut delight!

A few months after that, Danny's roommate moved out suddenly. I wondered why anyone would move out from such a generous guy.

I was soon to find out.

~

The very day Danny's roommate moved out, Danny stuck his head in my room and said, "Hey buddy, why don't you come and room with me?"

That was like music to my ears. "You bet, Danny," I said. And that night I moved into Danny's room.

It didn't take long before I understood why Danny's last roommate moved out.

In fact it started the first night. You see, I was the kind of student who really got stuck in and did my homework. No problem. I liked high school. And besides, I always thought, best get it all done and then I can have fun.

Danny? He wasn't like that at all. In fact, he hardly did any homework at all. Ever!

And something else was different. I liked to go to sleep around 9 pm. Sometimes I'd stay up until 10 pm. But hardly ever later than that. Why? Because I had a busy schedule. I had to work in the school bakery, go to class, do my homework, and play softball. All that sort of stuff.

Danny? He seemed to wake up at night and sleep in the day. Sometimes he'd just sleep right through his classes.

I'd never met anyone like Danny! I mean, even the craziest kids I knew went to class. I didn't realize sleeping all day was even an option!

I was fast asleep our first night, and that's when I found out why Danny was just so sleepy at class time. I was in the middle of a dream when Danny shook me awake. "James, James, wake up, I need your help!"

Danny needs my help? What for? Is there an emergency?

"I'm jumping out the window now," he said as if it were the most normal thing in the world, "and I'll be back in 45 minutes. I need you to lift me back into the dorm."

"What Danny, are you crazy?"

"No, trust me, this is really important, ok?"

And with that, he whipped our widow up letting in a blast of the winter air, and jumped out onto the snow below.

I was shocked. I'd never had a roommate who did anything like that!

～

I sort of dozed off, but about 45 minutes later there was a tapping on the window. I got up and looked out, and there below me in the snow was a man who looked like Santa Claus. He had a big sack on his back. A red beanie on his head. And clouds of white breath coming out of his nostrils. It's not easy walking through the snow carrying a heavy bag you know!

I opened the window and Danny looked up and smiled his mischievous grin. "Help me with this, will ya?" he said as he awkwardly handed the bag toward me. I reached down and pulled it through the window. It was a huge black trash bag. *That's really weird*, I thought.

"Can you help me back in now, buddy?" Danny said in a way that was more a command than a question.

I reached down and pulled him up as best as I could. All those donuts had made Danny a bit rolly polly, so it wasn't easy getting him back through the window. By the time he fell on our floor, we were both puffing and the freezing air was pouring in our wide-open window.

After pulling the window back in place, I turned to Danny and asked, "What on earth are you up to Danny?" He laughed and pointed towards the trash bag. But that didn't help make sense of things at all.

"What's in the bag, Danny?"

"Whaddaya think's in the bag?" he replied with a giggle. I looked at the big black trash bag, and said "Garbage?"

"You think I'd go trekking through mountains of snow to go pick up garbage. Do ya think I'm crazy?" I didn't want to reply, because in truth, at that moment, I was thinking he was a little nuts!

"Nah, I go to the donut shop to get the donuts!" Danny said with a chuckle.

I looked over at our clock; it was 3 a.m.

"Wow, the donut shop is still open at this time of night?" I asked surprised. "And they're selling donuts by the trash bag full? And you have special permission to go out and buy them?"

Danny began laughing. He laughed so hard his frizzy hair started shaking. His whole freckly face turned bright red.

"No, no, no!" he said, and snorted between giggles. "The donut shop isn't open! And no, they don't sell donuts in trash bags! And no, I don't have permission from anyone for anything!"

"Well, then, what on earth is going on?"

"I get the donuts from the trash behind the shop. They throw all the donuts they don't sell during the day into their trash dumpster out the back. See? I go to the dumpster, have a look inside the bags, and choose the one's filled with donuts. I get the donuts free. I sell them for a buck each. And I get all the profit!"

I was feeling a little ill at this point.

"You mean all those donuts you've given me the last few months, they all came from the dumpster?"

"Well...."

"And you picked them out from between the dirty paper towels, rotten tomatoes, the smelly old rags and the moldy cabbages?"

"Well...."

"And you never told me!"

"Well...."

"Well, what?"

"Well, James, how'd ya like a donut, buddy," Danny said as he motioned to the trash bag sitting between us on the floor.

"No, Danny, no thanks. I'm completely over your dumpster donuts!"

And you know what? I never ate another of Danny's dumpster donuts again. Not ever. And though all the other boys still came from all over the dorm for their sugary donut treats, I never even wanted one!

Why?

Because where stuff comes from really matters.

~

When I thought the donuts were coming from a nice clean donut shop display case, well I just wanted one of those sweet treats so badly. But as soon as I knew they were coming from a trash bag thrown into a dirty old dumpster?

No way!

It's a good rule of thumb - stuff is only as valuable as the place it comes from.

And in a way, the rule applies to all of us as well as donuts.

Some people think we come from the cosmic garbage heap. And somehow all this refuse kind of pulled together magically and we got stars and planets, our world with water and sunlight, and then, voila, we got life. And life magically became people.

So, here we are. A gigantic cosmic coincidence. Made from the galaxy's dumpster full of trash.

The problem? When you believe that, you don't tend to value people very highly. And, very sadly, there are lots of examples in history of those who believe people are made from the universe's garbage treating others very badly. There's the Nazis, of course. And also the Communists. They all believed humans were the product of the universe's garbage. And, very, very sadly, they treated people just like that.

And they had plenty of support from some of the smartest people on earth. Some scientists even said that different people evolved from different monkeys or at different rates. So, they said, you can be very horrible to some people because they aren't as evolved as other people are. Really, they said that! Isn't that awful?

Some people believed that since evolution produces the best results, we shouldn't care what happens to poor people because they are losers. And evolution is all about ensuring the winners win, and the losers are wiped out. It is a very cruel way to think!

Even today, some people think that if a person is very young or very old, well, their life just doesn't matter. Why? Because we're just made from the universe's garbage heap.

And maybe I'd feel the same way, if I believed that humans are a gigantic mistake.

But I don't. You see, there is overwhelming evidence that the universe has a great Designer. A Designer who carefully and precisely made our world so life could exist. And then brilliantly created life – including people just like you and me.

When we understand that God made us, well, we know we shouldn't treat people badly, because we're all brothers and sisters. And every person's life has to matter, Why? Because we all are made in the image of God.

That is why I am so thankful that I know that you and I come from a loving, caring, masterful God. Not from a cosmic trash pile like Danny's disgusting dumpster donuts!

~

Years after graduating from high school, I went back to visit my old school. Can you guess where I stopped for a snack?

You guessed it, the famous donut shop.

And can you guess where I went to get my donuts?

Did I go around the back to the dumpster to see if I could find a free donut in the trash?

No way!

I was happy to walk in and pick out a lovely fresh donut from the display case and pay for it in cash.

On that day, I chose the famous sour strawberry cream donut - light brown with sweet strawberry icing sugar on the outside and slightly sour strawberry cream inside. I sat down and ate that donut with relish. Oooh. It tingled on my tongue. I have to tell you. It was beautiful!

And where it came from? That made all the difference!

To see the recipe for sour cream strawberry donuts, visit:

www.brownroadbooks.com and click on the **Extras** button on the top menu - you'll be happy you did :)

Why Did I Go to a New High School?

I made a promise to you, and now I have to keep my word. Honestly, I'd rather not. But a promise is a promise, right?

The truth is, I got into a spot of trouble at my old boarding school in Singapore. I mean, I did nothing even close to what Danny did! But I did disagree with some of the people in charge of the school, and I did so in a way that was seen as disrespectful. Which, I suppose, it probably was. So, they said, "If you should so choose to came back for your senior year, you, Mr. Smarty Pants, will be on probation."

They didn't quite say it like that, but that was pretty much what they meant.

And you know what I thought? "I'd give anything not to have to go back to that school." And my mom and dad were cool with that. Which, looking back, was pretty amazing! I think they both knew that it was time for a change.

And you know what? They were right! Because I had the most wonderful year in Michigan - and the best part was all the new friends I made. What about Danny? We're still the best of friends! Even though, I never accept free donuts from him! No way!

How did skipping class work out for Danny? I'll tell you in the next story: "Disneyland's Back Door."

Disneyland's Back Door

D id you know that Disneyland has a back door? No? I didn't know either. Not until Roger told me. And, well, that was only the beginning of the trouble!

"Where are you going for spring break?" Roger asked me.

"Going? I'm going nowhere," I replied. "I mean, I've got nowhere to go. My parents are 9,000 miles away doing their medical missionary thing in Thailand. And me? Well, I'm stuck here at boarding school in the Michigan snow. So, Michigan it is."

"Stay in Michigan and do what?"

"Well, I haven't really thought about it..."

"Why don't you come to Los Angeles with me," Roger suggested casually. "I've got an uncle we can stay with. Plus, remember, Shane our buddy from boarding school in Singapore has moved to LA!"

Maybe I should have known better, but it sounded like a superb idea at the time. I'd saved up a little money from my bakery work.

If I could just find a very cheap ticket, I might just be able to pull it off.

~

Roger was my new roommate at my boarding school in Michigan. What had happened to Danny and his dumpster donuts?

Remember how Danny stayed up all night and slept all day? Well, that didn't go very well for him. When his report card arrived, he showed it to me. I looked at the first grade in the list and said, "Oh dear, Danny, that's not good at all." Then I looked at the last grade. And that one? No better. So I glanced at the middle. Yikes! From top to bottom it was F's in every direction!

"I can't believe they've given me all F's," said Danny indignantly.

"Well, Danny, I mean, you haven't gone to class for quite awhile, and when you do, you go to sleep on your desk, and you don't put in your home work, and…"

"It's really not at all fair!" exclaimed Danny as if I'd not said anything at all.

Well, you can be the judge of whether it was fair or not. But the school said that if you are a student, you simply have to show up to class and do your work. "You can have a lot of fun here, Danny," the principal said, "but you can't *only* have fun!"

That didn't seem right to Danny, she he dropped out of high school, moved back in with his parents and began flipping burgers for a living. Sometimes he'd call me and ask how dorm life was going. I'd tell him, and then he'd give a big sigh. I think he missed it. And, to be honest, I really missed Danny.

~

Just when I was feeling lonely, who should show up in Michigan but my old friend Roger from Singapore.

When he arrived, I said, "Roger, what on earth are you doing here in Michigan?"

"Well," said Rog, "I got into a spot of trouble at our school in Singapore." I nodded my head understanding. I knew it was very easy to get into trouble at that school. "So," Roger continued, "I went back to Pakistan where my parents are missionaries and went to the American school there." I nodded my head understandingly some more.

And then he was quiet.

"Yeah, so you were in Pakistan at the American school, so why are you here?" I was mystified.

"Well, you see James, I got into a spot of trouble there, too."

"Roger, you're kidding me, right?" I blurted out. "Are you telling me you had to leave two different high schools in one year?"

Roger mumbled something I couldn't understand, and then he said, "So I wonder if I can move in and be your new roommate?"

I didn't know exactly what to say. As much as I missed Danny, I was quite happy to have less craziness around me. But how could I say no to Roger. I mean, we were missionary kid buddies. And you just don't turn your back on a buddy like that, do you? "Sure, Rog," I replied with a forced smile.

You might think that when Danny moved out, things might have calmed down. But that wasn't how it worked at all. If anything, Roger was even crazier than Danny. We called him "Roger the Dodger" as he was always up to some kind of mischief.

The simple truth was, where Roger went, trouble followed. And I was about to find out why.

~

When we left Michigan it was cold, and there were piles of snow all around. What a different world we found when we walked out of Los Angeles airport. The sun was blasting down, the sky was blue and our friend Shane bounced up to us wearing shorts, boat shoes and a t-shirt. Wow, LA was going to be great!

Shane took us to his convertible black VW Golf GTI with a red stripe down the side. I was really impressed. Even though I was a senior in high school, I didn't even have a drivers license - let alone a fast, cool car! Shane put the top down, and soon we were zooming along the LA freeways with the wind in our hair, on our way to meet Roger's family.

Roger's family were about the nicest people on earth. They just set us up, fed us, and let us do whatever we wanted to. They treated us like adults.

Which, thinking back, might have been a mistake!

Why? Because Roger had an idea.

"Why don't we go to Disneyland tomorrow?" he asked.

"Aren't we a little bit too old for Disneyland?" replied Shane, who had been in California all of eight months and was already pretending to be bored with everything in Los Angeles.

"Nah. They've got great rides there - Space Mountain, the Matterhorn, Pirates of the Caribbean... Come on, its Disneyland - it'll be fantastic!" proclaimed Roger enthusiastically.

"But Rog," I said, "I've got a problem. I blew all my cash on the ticket out here and Disneyland's super expensive."

"No problem," said Roger, "I've got a way to get in free."

~

"You've got complementary tickets?" I asked Roger.

"Well, you can sort of call it that, if you like," he replied with a laugh. "We'll just go through Disneyland's back door."

"There's a back door to Disneyland?" I asked surprised.

"Sure is, and I'll show ya how to open it James, me boy!" said Roger with a big chuckle.

The next morning at breakfast, Roger announced, "Eat up big, coz we have a busy day ahead of us!"

Grace, Roger's sister, leaned in and asked suspiciously, "What kind of busy day, Roger?"

Roger just ignored her. He was a bit like that. If he didn't like what you had to say, he pretended he didn't hear you.

She looked over at me. I've got to admit, Grace was super-nice. And you know, I sort of had a weakness for super-nice girls.

"James, what are you guys planning?"

"Oh, well, we're off to Disneyland," Grace nodded as I talked. "But we're going in the back door…"

Grace nodded again, and then asked, "Whatdaya mean, back door?"

"I'm not sure, Grace, Roger knows about it."

At this point Roger was scowling at me.

I shrugged my shoulders.

Grace looked over at Roger, "What are you up to this time, Rog?"

"Hey, nothing Grace. Just mind your own business."

"I can smell a rat, Rog, you better come clean!"

Roger was getting upset. It was written all over his face. I could tell things were going to get complicated very soon, so I jumped in. "Hey Grace, why don't you just come with us?"

She laughed, and simply said, "Sure!"

Roger looked at me and shook his head in disappointment while he rolled his eyes. But at least the two stopped bickering.

As we walked out to Shane's car, he turned around and said, "Why'd ya have to get Grace into this?"

I just let out a sigh in reply. But the truth was, I was really glad she was coming along! Grace was cool. And I liked her.

We were back on LA's freeways driving to Disneyland when Roger laid out the plan.

"Here's the deal. There's a fence all around Disneyland, coz they want you to go in the front."

"Right," I nodded.

"But there's a back door, see?"

"What do you mean?" said Shane.

"Yeah, a back door. Lots of kids around LA know about the back door. My cousin told me about it. And the great thing about the back door? If you go in that way, Disneyland is totally free!"

"That's weird," I said, "Is it some kind of special deal for LA kids?"

"Well, sort of," said Roger laughing again.

When we arrived at Disneyland, we didn't park in the Disney parking lots near the entrance. Instead we parked miles away. And then we began our unusual trip to Disney's back door.

It was, in truth, a mad trip. Over busy roads, under barriers, past shaggy bushes and rough ledges. All of this, just to arrive outside a very high wire-mesh fence.

"What's this about?" demanded Grace who wasn't impressed at all by Roger's planning. "There's no door here!"

I looked at the fence and thought exactly the same thing. There was one thing for sure - no one was going over that fence!

"Just follow me," instructed Roger, "and you'll see..."

So we began our march around the perimeter of Disneyland. As we walked we caught a few glimpses of a Disney building every now and again. The bright sunshine that had seemed so wonderful the day before, became unbearably hot. I was sweating. And I was so thirsty!

"How much further?" I asked.

"Just a little bit," Roger replied in the tone of an irritated parent.

And sure enough, in just a couple minutes he announced, "We've arrived."

I looked around and didn't see any door at all. "What do you mean, 'arrived?'" I asked.

"Just watch this," instructed Roger.

He walked over to the point where the steel mesh fence met a tall metal pole, and with a quick flick of his hand he peeled it back, creating a small, but passable opening.

"See, some kids used wire cutters down here. Now all we gotta do is crawl through, and we're in Disneyland!"

I looked at the crack a little horrified and a little intrigued. Wow, just a bit of a wiggle, and we're in Disneyland. For free! But, man, this is sure to be a terrible idea!

We were right by a super busy road. Cars were flying by on all sides. Wouldn't someone see us? Wouldn't we get caught?

There was no time for thinking. Roger had already squeezed through. Shane was right behind him, Grace not far behind, and that just left me.

I looked both ways, and then I followed. The wire ends were jagged, and one caught my t-shirt and ripped a nasty hole as I crawled through. Still, it was a great relief to be inside the park, and sur-rounded by small trees.

"Let's get to the top and see where we are," said Roger.

We scampered up as fast as we could, but as soon as we came to the crest Roger whispered urgently, "Get your heads down!"

And for good reason. Just at that moment the Disneyland wild west steam train came chugging along just below us.

I saw a kid pointing at us. I wonder what she was saying to her mom. Maybe something like, "Look mom, there are kids in those bushes."

"Oh don't be silly darling…"

"No really mom, look." The mom looked up at us.

We ducked.

"Oh, I think they're just actors, darling, pretending to be bandits…"

After the train passed, Roger said urgently, "We've got to get into the crowd and mix as quickly as possible. Disneyland has surveillance everywhere. If they see us running across the train tracks and over the wall, they'll nab us, and we'll be in big, big trouble."

"Maybe we should just leave the way we came," I suggested.

"Don't be dopey," said Roger, "we've made it this far - we have to go on!"

Looking back, I don't think my idea was dopey at all! In fact, what we did next was pretty foolish!

∽

The four of us ran across the tracks like scared rabbits, hopped a little wall as people looked at us like we were mad, and before you knew it, we were part of the immense crowd swirling outside "It's a Small World."

Looking at all those innocent little children about to get on that sweet ride I felt rotten. There was their lovely innocence. And us? We were being pretty nasty, really.

But that feeling didn't last long.

Soon we were off on the fastest, highest, most exciting rides.

We jumped on the Matterhorn roller-coaster. It was terrific fun. And as soon as one ride finished, we lined up and went again. We must have flashed past the Abominable Snowman roaring at us at least five times! By the end, we were yelling "faster" at every turn.

Then we moved onto Space Mountain, where we sat in the darkness, ready for our thrilling space adventure over and over again. We sat at the front, we yelled the loudest and we laughed the longest.

Every thrilling moment washed away my tinge of guilt.

We stayed and rode the rides until midnight, when Disneyland closed. And then we walked right out the front door like everyone else.

"We really got our money's worth out of Disneyland today," cracked Roger. We all laughed, and laughed and laughed. But as much as we laughed, it didn't cover a bad taste in my mouth.

～

It was many years later that I woke up at night. And I started thinking about Disneyland's back door. I smirked to myself about Roger and how crazy he was. And how we'd put one over on Disneyland. But the more I thought about it, something else popped into my head. I mean, it was a crazy adventure, but something just didn't feel right. In fact, it felt really wrong.

Then I thought, *We didn't take anything from anyone and we never got caught. So what's the problem?*

Besides, it's not like the Disney Corporation needs my money! Their CEO makes millions and millions every year. Why should I contribute to him and the rest of the Disney fat cats?

Besides, if I'd had to pay, I wouldn't have gone. So it's not like they would have gotten cash from ticket sales to me if I hadn't snuck in. Right?

And the lines at Disneyland rides are too long. The food is too expensive. And the crowds are too large. Why should anyone pay good money to be forced to stand in line most of the time they're in the park? Plus, they used every trick in the trade to market the place. They made me want to go!

And, even if all that wasn't true, it was just a bit of fun. An adventure. No one got hurt. So what's the problem?

But then I thought about it another way.

It's their park. They have to pay for everything that goes into operating it. Which, when you think about it, must be a lot of money. They have to pay the cleaners, the performers, the engineers, the designers, the decorators, and everyone else. How can they do that if everyone sneaks in?

There are a thousands of other places we could have gone for free. But we chose to go to Disneyland. Doesn't Disneyland have the right to set the entrance fee and expect visitors to pay it?

The rides and the experience is their product. Just as much so as, say, a smart phone or a hotdog is a product.

Would I ever lean over a hotdog stand, grab a hotdog, and run off?

No, never! That would be stealing, and I'm no thief.

I'd certainly never take someone's smartphone. Only a dishonest person would do something like that.

And I'm certainly not dishonest!

Or am I?

I tried to forget that thought. Which was easy to do, because I was busy. But when I woke up the next night again, it kind of bugged me. It almost felt like my conscience was speaking to me.

One day I got tired of thinking about it. So I decided to do something about it.

~

I sat down and wrote a letter to Disneyland. I looked up the entrance fee. I put double the amount of the entrance fee in the letter and I sent it off.

And that was that.

And I've never felt bad about it again.

I know what we did was wrong. I shouldn't have done it. So I tried to make it right. Not to earn God's forgiveness, but because I felt it was the right thing to do.

Of course, sometimes we do the wrong thing in a way we can't undo. And maybe our greatest wrongs are the ones no one has the power to correct. Think of Paul in the Bible. He helped kill innocent people before he was converted. How do you ever fix that? But God forgave him. That's the point of grace.

But, when there's something we can do to make things right, it sure feels good to do it. Like Zacchaeus, the tax collector, who ripped people off. When Jesus came to his house, Zachaeus decided to give back all the money he'd stollen - and a lot more too. I think I know just a little bit of how great Zacchaeus must have felt after that. Like a weight was lifted off his shoulders and he was free again!

Last summer I went to Disneyland with my youngest daughter. We had a terrific time together. The Matterhorn was even more fun with her next to me screaming! And the fireworks? I can hardly describe how spectacular they were!

When I think back on our trip, all I have are good memories. I don't have even an ounce of guilt. Because this time, we didn't go through Disneyland's back door. We bought our tickets and we walked right in the front door. And it felt terrific!

If you'd like to read a story I wrote about Walt Disney, visit:

www.brownroadbooks.com and click on the **Extras** button on the top menu - it's a terrific bonus story :)

Forgive or Forget?

If I had to be honest, when I went to school I had no friends.

It wasn't that I was unfriendly. Unkind. Or uninterested.

It was worse than that.

I had no friends because I literally had *no* friends.

I went to a school for missionary children on the tropical island of Penang, Malaysia. And there just weren't that many of us. In fact, there were only nine kids in the whole school, and all the other kids were older than me. I was the only one in my class.

It was the worst!

And then, like a miracle, one day that all changed.

I was riding my bike home from school, when a car slowed down next to me and I looked in the window. There, looking right back at me, was a boy my age. He had light blond hair, bright blue eyes, and a shy smile. I waved at him, and he half waved back at me.

Wow, I thought, wouldn't it be cool to have a friend like him.

I didn't think too much more about it as I peddled on in the hot sun, because I'd never seen him before and I expected I'd never see him again.

When I got home I noticed something strange. There was a big van at the house across the street.

"What's going on?" I asked my mom.

"Oh, Jamie, a new family is moving in," answered my mom, "and you're going to be very surprised by who they are."

"Why?" I asked. "Just go over and see for yourself," was her mysterious response.

⁓

The home across the street was so big, it looked like a hotel. And it had the longest driveway you could imagine. The two big iron gates at the front were usually bolted shut. So I'd never actually been to the house - and I was very nervous to go now. As I walked passed the gates, I felt very small. In fact, it took all the bravery I had not to turn around and run back to our home.

Then I noticed something incredible. There, right next to the moving truck was the same car that had passed by me with the waving boy.

Could it really be?

Before I could answer that question, I heard a voice with a thick Scottish accent, "Who's this wee little fella coming down my drive?" I looked over, and there was a big, strong man, with dark blond curly hair and piercing blue eyes looking at me. I was very scared, but then his face broke into a big smile.

"Your mom told me to expect a visit from you," the man continued in an accent so strong I could barely understand him. Still, I felt relived, and, without thinking, blurted out, "Do you have a boy?"

"Aye, I certainly do," he said, "come with me, and let me introduce you to my Alex."

As we walked in the front door, there he was. The blond boy who had waved to me. He was smiling shyly. And I felt rather awkward. You know, that sort of "what do I say now" sort of feeling?

"I saw you on your bike," said Alex.

"And I saw you in the car," I replied.

And then we both laughed because what we'd just said was so obvious it seemed ridiculous. And from there, we glided comfortably into all the important things in life. And it turned out we had a lot in common. What did we love the most? Cars. Fast cars. Cool cars. Hot cars. Funky cars. We loved them all!

We played with our toy cars. We raced slot cars. We looked at pictures of cars. We watched racing cars on TV. We even went to stunt car show that was totally awesome.

And boy did we have a lot of fun. We went to a waterfall in the jungle and leapt off rocks into the water. We went to the beach and swam in the crystal clear ocean. We went to the market and looked at toys, pets and more toys. We ate the best food in the world at little roadside stands. We rode our bikes everywhere. We even put together a bike show based on the tricks we'd seen at the car stunt show. It was just the best time you could ever have.

I wasn't Jamie with no friends on earth any more. I was Jamie, with my best friend in the world. His name was Alex. He was from Scotland. And he was the coolest kid I'd ever met.

Everything was just going along as well as a friendship could. Until...

~

Until one day I got a call. It was Alex, and he was very excited: "Jamie, you've got to come over as fast as you can. Don't walk, ride your bike. And ride as fast as you possibly can. It's urgent!"

I didn't ask what the fuss was all about. Why would I? Alex said it was urgent, so it must be! I just jumped on my bike and began to pedal furiously. I shot past Alex's huge iron gates and flew down his enormous twisting driveway.

And then, all of a sudden, my bike shook, shot up in the air, and I went flying over the handlebars and came to an almighty crash onto the boiling hot, rough driveway. As I lay there whimpering in pain, Alex and his brother Rob appeared from the bushes on either side of the driveway laughing.

"You should have seen the look on your face," Alex said, struggling to get the words out of his mouth, he was laughing so hard. Rob was doubled over laughing. "We really surprised you this time!" he chortled.

But I wasn't laughing. My knees and elbows were all scraped up, I had a cut on my hand that was starting to bleed, and my head had taken a big knock. As they ran towards me giggling, they must have all of a sudden realized what they'd done.

"Oh, Jamie, are you hurt?" Alex asked. I was in so much pain I couldn't answer, instead I just started crying. Not little tears, but big sobs. And it wasn't just because I was bleeding and hurting all over; it was because I couldn't believe my best friend in the world had done this to me!

Alex and Rob fussed around me, looking very guilty. "But, um, it did seem like a funny idea, and, ah, your face really was surprised, um, but, ah," Alex stammered.

I wasn't interested in what he had to say. All I wanted to do was to get back on my feet and go home. It took me a minute, but I struggled up. "Do you want me to walk you back home?" asked Alex apologetically.

"No Alex, I want you to leave me alone!" I said as I turned my back and hobbled with my bike toward home.

～

When I got home my mom met me at the door. "What's happened to you?" she said in a very concerned voice.

"I've had a terrible fall off my bike, and its all Alex's fault!" I told her.

After a bath, I was sitting in my pajamas with bandaids on my many cuts and scratches, when my mom asked me for the whole story. I told her everything.

"Alex isn't my friend any more! He's a rotten kid. The worst kid I've ever known!" I concluded.

"Hmm, that's not good at all," she said.

I'm not sure what she did, but not too long after there was a knock at our door. My mom went to open it as I remained in my room. Soon she was back.

"Alex's come to see you," she said simply.

"Well tell him to go away!" I blurted out.

"Are you sure that's the answer you want to give?"

"Why not?" I pointed at my cuts "I've had it with that kid!"

"Well, what he did was very careless," agreed my mom, "but remember, sometimes kids don't think everything through before they do it. I know Alex pretty well now, and I can't imagine him doing this trick if he understood how painful the results would be. My guess is he just did it, without thinking carefully. Remember, he's been a great friend - think of all the fun you've had together."

"Well, sure, we've had some fun..."

"Has he ever been disloyal or mean to you?"

"Well, no, I can't say he has."

"Do you think he's worth forgiving?"

I'd never really thought about forgiveness that way. I mean, my parents had always taught me to forgive everyone - even mean people who deliberately do the wrong thing. Now my mom was putting a value on forgiveness. It kind of shocked me.

"What do you mean?" I asked.

"This is the way I think about it," my mom said. "It can be hard to find real friends in life. But no matter how good our friends are, sometime or another, they'll hurt us. And no matter how well intentioned we are, we'll hurt them. It's just the way human beings are." She paused for a minute while I thought about what she'd said.

"So," she continued, "we have to make a decision; are our friends worth forgiving? Because if they aren't, they aren't really friends - they're just people we know who we hang out with until they do something that hurts us, and then we walk away from them."

I sat on the edge of my bed, aching all over. Was Alex my friend? Of course he was... In fact, he was the best friend I'd ever had. But still, he'd also really hurt me. And he had no right to do that. But was he worth forgiving? I was conflicted.

Eventually I looked up at my mom and said, "You're right. If we're supposed to even forgive our enemies, I suppose we must forgive our friends. Even when they do really hurtful things. But it isn't easy!"

My mom smiled, "Sometimes forgiving friends is actually harder than forgiving enemies because the people we love can hurt us the most. But it is the right thing to do."

We walked out to the front door where Alex stood, looking down at the ground. He seemed small framed in the large open doorway. When I got closer, I realized he was crying. And that made me feel sick. Without even looking at me, he began to speak: "I am so, so sorry Jamie."

Wow, the way he said it, I knew he really meant it.

"Hey Alex," I said softly, "I forgive you." The words just tumbled out easily. I mean, how could I not forgive him? He was, after all, my very best friend ever.

He looked up and smiled. And I smiled too. It was like a big burden had been lifted off both of us. Even my cuts and bruises didn't hurt so much after that!

The funny thing is this: if we'd been friends before that, we were even better friends after. We'd faced a real test of friendship, and somehow we'd made it through. And that made our friendship much deeper and stronger. Something really bad had turned into something very good. How weird is that?

It wasn't all that long after the bike debacle that my dad came home with big news. "We're going home!" he said.

"What do you mean, we're going home?" I asked. "We are home!"

"I mean we're going home to Australia," he said.

Home to Australia? I was only two years old when we'd left Australia for our island home in Malaysia. This island was my home now. And besides, I had no friends at all in Australia. And here on our island? I had the best friend in the world!

My last memory of Alex was looking out of the window of the car rolling out our driveway towards the airport for the move back to Australia. There was Alex, and I don't think I've ever seen a sadder looking kid. And I felt just as sad inside. For good reason. I never saw my best friend Alex ever again.

Until...

~

Until last year when, after a long search, I found Alex and sent him an email. I wondered if he'd even remember me. And if he did, would he bother to write back?

The next day I got a note that started: "Yes, Jamie, its me, your best friend Alex!" He was overjoyed we were back in contact after all these years. And, of course, so was I. I just sat looking at his note and reading it over and over again. I could not believe my eyes. It was too good to be true!

It turns out Alex is now a famous newspaper reporter in London, England. Can you guess what he writes about? Come on, what do you think Alex writes about? Politics? No. The weather? Nope! Maybe art? Nah. Alex writes about cars. Fast cars. Cool cars. Hot cars. Funky cars. Alex's life is all wrapped up in cars. If you want to know if we still have anything in common now that we're all grown up, you should read the story in the book entitled "Lambo in Paris." That might give you a hint!

Alex wrote and said, "Please come and visit me in London!"

So guess what I did? I happened to be going to Europe and I arranged a stop in London.

When I arrived there, I took a black London taxi to a nice old English townhouse not too far from all the things you know - Big Ben, Tower Bridge, Buckingham Palace.

When I jumped out of the taxi, I looked at Alex's home. It was very quaint, with roses twisting up the side and pretty English Bluebells next to some happy yellow flowers. As I walked up the short path to the front door I felt really nervous. I mean, it had been so many years since I'd seen Alex. What would he be like? Would we have anything to say to each other? Now that he's famous, would he be too proud for his old friend?

I shouldn't have worried at all because when the door opened, there was Alex and he let out whoop, and as he gave me a big hug he said, "I saw on the bike!" And do you know what I replied? "I saw in the car!" And then we laughed and laughed and laughed.

It was just one of the most wonderful experiences of my entire life. It is like something very precious that I lost as a child had been given back to me.

So, are friends worth forgiving? If you could feel the warmth I have in my heart as I write this story you'd know the answer: Yes! Yes! Yes! A thousand times, yes!

So let's forgive our enemies. That's the right thing to do. But let's not forget to also forgive our friends. It can be even harder to do. Because our friends can hurt us even more than our enemies. But forgiveness is the most wonderful gift God has given to us. And the benefits last a lifetime. Trust me. I have a friend to prove it!

Stinky Fruit

Alex and I loved to go to shopping. No, not to a supermarket or a shopping mall. We went to a real market. Where flies buzzed around the meat, the fish stank in the sun, and the open drains smelled like - well, like open drains do! But of course, that's not why we loved the market. We loved it because it was just such a fascinating place. I'll tell you more about it in "Monkey Mischief." But before I get there, I better tell you about the stinky fruit.

As gross as the meat was in the hot air, the fruit and vegetables at the market were terrific. There were all kinds of fruit that you can hardly find outside of Asia. For example, there were piles of bright red rambutans, with their soft spiky hairs on the outside that feel a little like plastic. Don't worry, that's not the part you eat! Inside is a sweet, clear fruit that is the perfect treat on a hot day. And then there are mangosteens - smooth dark purple on the outside and pure juicy white on the inside.

But the king of the fruit, no doubt, is the durian. Durian is the "stinky fruit" which, believe it or not, smells even worse than the fish, meat and the drains combined, but tastes like a little bit of heaven.

There really is no fruit in the world quite like durian. In fact, it is unique among any fruit, vegetable, grain or manufactured food of any kind I've ever seen, anywhere! If you were going to make up a fruit, this is about as far from anything anyone would ever dream of creating. When I describe it, I think you'll understand what I'm saying.

First, it's big - sometimes as big as two American footballs combined. And heavy. Just one durian will weigh you down. But it gets worse.

Durians are covered in big green spikes that really hurt if they knock against you. It almost looks like a cruel medieval weapon. And if you ever have the misfortune of walking under a durian tree when a durian falls down, well, you'd have a very bad day indeed!

But even all of this isn't the most remarkably bad thing about the durian.

The worst thing is that, when you cut them open, they smell like nothing you have ever smelt before. Unless, of course, you have a particularly stinky brother! Not only is it pungent, but the smell is super strong. And when you eat them, the smell gets on your breath. You never need to guess who has just eaten durian, you just need to use your nose and you'll know who!

So, you might think at this point, that durian is something to stay well clear of.

But that is the strange thing.

Durian is wonderful. And I'm not teasing here, it really is!

As crazy as this sounds, durian is one of the tastiest things you can ever eat. Inside are off-white creamy custardy flesh surrounding smooth light brown seeds. The creamy flesh just melts in your mouth. And the flavor? It is a true delicacy.

Now if I try to describe the flavor to you, you'll say, "That's disgusting!" And I get it. If someone told me about it, I'd say you have to be mad to eat something like that. But here I am, telling you in all truth, it is marvelous stuff.

Even if it does stink like a thousand dirty toilets. And even if it does taste a little bit like garlic tinged sweet creamy custard. And even if, once you've eaten it, you'll smell like a sewer for the rest of the day. Truly, if you get the chance, you've got to give durian a try...

Uncle Dan & the Exploding Volcano

You may never have visited the island of Tanna, or maybe you haven't even heard of it. It's a place so marvelous and magical that you may not believe me that it's real. Uncle Dan almost didn't. But that was before Uncle Dan and I flew on a jet from Australia to Vanuatu, and then we took a little propeller plane all the way down to the tiny island of Tanna with its dangerous center.

We were on a mission trip.

Well, it wasn't your normal mission trip. We didn't build any schools or give anyone any medical treatment. Just as well. Uncle Dan doesn't know anything about giving injections and you certainly wouldn't want to live in a house he made – it might fall down!

What Uncle Dan is super good at, is making videos. But not just any kind of videos – videos that tell the story about missions. Why is this important? Well, those videos are sent to churches all around the world so they can learn about how to help clinics, schools and all the other great things the church does.

So, while Uncle Dan isn't much good at actually building schools or treating patients, his videos contain the stories that inspire people across the globe to give the money necessary that keeps all that stuff going.

And that's why Uncle Dan had come to Tanna. He was making a video about clinics many miles from anywhere that provide the only healthcare to kids just like you. Important? You bet they are!

But there is one thing you should know about Tanna. Yes, it has beautiful beaches. Of course it has fabulous coral reefs. Coconuts? Yes, everywhere! Crabs so big they make your eyes bulge out when you see them? Yep! And what about children? Yes - the loveliest kids on earth. But that isn't what I'm talking about.

I'm talking about the VOLCANO!

Not just a normal, old quiet volcano, but one that spits red-hot lava all over the place. You know that lava is melted rocks, right? That volcano groans with mighty groans, it explodes with mighty explosions, and when it blows, it really blows!

～

Uncle Dan was interested in visiting the volcano.

He said, "We should go and take a look." I said, "Maybe we should stay away." "No," said Uncle Dan, "we should definitely go." I said, "Maybe we should definitely stay away?" Uncle Dan said, "That settles it then, we're off to see the mighty volcano - at night!"

So up to the volcano we went. Can I tell you the truth? I wasn't very keen to stand next to an exploding volcano. That just doesn't sound like a good idea to me. What do you think?

Anyway, Uncle Dan said he isn't afraid of anything – not even boiling hot lava!

When we got to the edge of the volcano there were some other people who were there gawking over the edge. People are weird aren't they – they could do anything at all, and the best thing they could think to do was to run up to the edge of an exploding volcano – that's crazy!

I decided that, well, since I was there I should get a better view – does that make me a little crazy too? So I began walking on a little track on the lip of the volcano up to the highest point. It's hard to be cautious when you're curious!

I was almost to the top when all of a sudden, whoosh, wallop, bang, kaboom! The volcano exploded and up shot red-hot molten lava high above my head! But, fortunately, not right above my head – it was over to the side a little. That kind of made my heart jump into my throat! But still, I thought, I'd go a little higher. And that's when the volcano exploded all over again, but this time much bigger. The lava looked like it filled the sky above me!

You know when you play baseball or cricket and someone hits a ball high in the air and you have to figure out exactly where it's going to fall and run over and catch it? Some people are super good at that. I'm not one of them. I can't tell where that ball is going to fall, so I run all over the place trying to get in exactly the right spot. But I never seem to be able to.

That was exactly what it was like with the lava. Except that instead of wanting to catch it, I wanted very much NOT to catch it! I looked up, I looked down, I moved my legs this way and that, like a crab zig-zagging across a beach. Before I knew it, those huge balls of lumpy lava had splashed down – but not on me.

Well, that was enough of volcanoes for me! I scurried down the path again as quick as my knobbly legs could take me.

But, and this is important, Uncle Dan didn't come down. He just kept going up right to the top of the volcano rim and all the time he carried his big video camera, tripod, and all his gear.

~

When I got back to the bottom of the rim, I met a group of people. They were all wearing little plastic helmets. I asked, "Why are you wearing plastic helmets?"

"Because there's red hot lava shooting up above us," said a man with a strong French accent.

I must of looked at them kind of funny.

And then he said said, "Oui, we know you are thinking, a little plastic helmet won't protect us from boiling hot lava."

How did they know that was exactly what I was thinking?

I asked the group why they didn't join Uncle Dan at the top of the volcano.

"Well," said the man, "we arrived here three hours ago and we were going to go up to that spot, but just then the volcano shot lava out and it landed in exactly the spot where your friend is now! So we would prefer to watch from here…"

Uncle Dan – come down now! I thought, but I wasn't about to run all the way back up that ridge. No way!

Uncle Dan is a bit of a daredevil. He stayed up there. Then there was a huge explosion, and lava fell all over the place. Even brave Uncle Dan couldn't ignore that. He packed up and I think I saw him scurrying as quickly as he could down from the rim.

I think so, but later he said I didn't. When he came down you know what he said to me? "How's my scared little friend doing?" Ooooh, that made me squirm because, you see, I am very big and I normally think I'm quite brave. Uncle Dan laughed and I had to laugh too because it was true, I was a little bit scared! And for good reason!

But then I told Uncle Dan the story about the hot lava raining down right where he had been standing. "Why didn't you tell me!" he said.

"Because you are so manly and brave that you wouldn't care!" I replied. And then we both laughed all over again because we knew that wasn't true!

I took some photos of the lava shooting up, but they're a bit blurry. "That's because," said Uncle Dan, "you were running like a little boy so fast away from the volcano when you took them!" By the way, that's not even true! And Uncle Dan took some really fabulous video. One day that clip will be in a mission video that people from New York to Nairobi, from Bangkok to Brisbane, from London to Los Angeles will see.

By the way, I've been thinking. You know, Uncle Dan has never done a surgery and he's never built a hospital, right? But the money his videos help raise has done a lot of both. So, you could say, I suppose, Uncle Dan has built a lot of schools and helped a lot of sick people – all using a video camera!

Want to see the exploding volcano that Uncle Dan filmed and some other pictures from Tanna? Visit: www.brownroadbooks.com and click on the **Extras** button on the top menu - it's an amazing island!

Lamborghini in Paris

Have you ever played spotto? You know the game where the first person to call out "spotto" when they see a yellow car wins.

I like to play spotto with my girls. But we don't play it like everyone else. You see, we have innovations and derivations. If the car is not only yellow, but super cool or very interesting, we declare it is a "spotto with laurels." If the car is yellow, but exceptionally boring, well, then it's a "spotto dud."

What kind of car gets laurels? Well, take the very yellow, very brash Porsche Carrera S Cabriolet that sped by us when we were on the way to school from our home by the beach the other morning. That's a very long name for a very fast car. And you know what cabriolet means don't you? It means its a convertible - and I love convertibles. So a convertible yellow Porsche with the top down definitely gets "spotto with laurels" from us!

But to get laurels, at least in our books, the yellow car doesn't have to be very fast; it can also be very funky. Take the old dusty yellow Citroën 2CV. It's an old French car that looks a little like a bug made of folded paper – and it almost is! But when you see one, it makes you smile – maybe because its front lights look a little like funny eyes at the end of antennae!

Recently I had a very big birthday. It was grand.

Cake? Yep.

Friends? Yep?

Balloons, cards and presents? Yes, Yes, Yes!

But there was something else.

You see, this birthday, my wife gave me a very special present. She said I could go to Paris. And not just go to Paris. But drive any car I like while there.

Seriously?

Do I have the best wife in the world!

~

I flew to London and visited Alex, and then I went to Paris on the Eurostar train that goes through the huge tunnel between London and Paris. That train goes 300 KPH – that's almost 200 MPH. The whole world looked a little blurry as we sped by!

When I arrive in Paris I walk over to the Place de la Concorde. During the French Revolution, they chopped people's heads off right there - including the heads of King Louis and Queen Marie

Antoinette. That's pretty awful, isn't it? If you want to know more about that, read the story in this book entitled "The Most Beautiful House in the World."

But I'm not here to think about headless kings and queens. I'm here because I'm about to walk up the Avenue des Champs-Élysées – which is very famous for its fancy shops.

But I'm not here to shop, either.

Or sightsee.

I'm not even here to eat at one of the famous restaurants.

No, I'm here to drive a car.

But not just any car.

I'm here to drive a convertible Lamborghini. But I've got a surprise coming. You see, when I arrive where my rental car is parked, I find out it isn't cool black, or fiery red, as I'd hoped, and it isn't a technical grey or pure white. No. This Lambo is the brightest yellow you can imagine!

I look at it and yell "SPOTTO!!!" Not just with laurels. This is the "ULTIMATE SPOTTO". You simply can't get more spotto than this! And that it's in the middle of Paris? Wow! And that I'm about to jump into the driver's seat and take it for a spin? I'm in another world!

I settle in the seat, and Pierre gets in the passenger seat. "I've got something very special for you Chames," he says. He calls me

"Chames" instead of "James" - I don't know why. I think it's his thick French accent. Anyway, I don't really care - everything sounds better in a French accent! And I'm in the driver's seat of a bright yellow Lamborghini in Paris. How awesome is that?

"Let's go!" Pierre says. I'm happy to comply, and we roar off down the avenue, weaving through the traffic back toward Place de la Concorde. Then Pierre yells "Turn right Chames." I swerve to the right, and we're speeding down along the Seine River. We come to a couple of tunnels. Pierre calls out, "No speed cameras in the tunnel, Chames, floor it, floor it!" I comply. The hair stands up on the back of my neck. The noise is deafening. The speed electrifying. The wind is buffeting us back and forth!

As we exit the second tunnel Pierre barks, "Sharp left, sharp left!" I swerve to the left and there in front of me silhouetted against the afternoon sun is the Eiffel Tower. As soon as we cross the Seine River, Pierre calls, "U-Turn!" I'm not sure if you can actually do that? Too late. Just did. And back we fly toward the Arc de Triomphe.

You know the Arc de Triomphe, don't you? It's that huge victory arch built by Napoleon in the middle of Paris. I think he built it a little too soon. As, when it was still under construction, Napoleon was defeated at Waterloo - and that was the end of him and all his "triomphes"!

We come to the arch and Pierre calls, "Go around, go around!" We fly around the traffic circle that surrounds the enormous arch. Avenues fly off like the spokes of a wheel in every direction. "Go left, Chames, left!" I throw the sharp yellow nose of the Lambo to the left, and, voila, we're back onto the Avenue des Champs-Élysées.

When we come to a stop, the sweat is running down the back of my neck, my hands are clammy and my heart is still racing. What a car! What a city! What a thrill!

~

The Lamborghini isn't the only nice car I've driven. In fact, driving fast cars is a little bit of a guilty pleasure I enjoy. I like the design. I like the sound. And most of all, I like the feeling of being caught halfway between great fun and total terror.

The interesting thing about beautifully fast cars is this: they can teach us a lot of lessons that are really worth knowing.

For example, the nicer the car, the more complicated the care.

When I picked up the Aston Martin V12 Vantage in England, I was told the front spoiler – which swoops very low indeed – gets damaged easily. So I must drive very, very carefully over bumps. And what if I don't? A new carbon fibre spoiler costs literally thousands of British pounds!

Of course, just minutes after I was told that, I came to a street with the hugest speed bumps I'd ever seen! Oh boy, was I ever careful. In fact, I went so slow that some high school kids walking by started pointing at me and laughing, "Look at that guy in that super hot car, and he's being overtaken by people on bicycles!" they laughed. Well, I just didn't care, because there's nothing cool about knocking the front spoiler off a super car - or having to buy a new one!

Super cars require super care. It's just that way.

So when I stopped to fill up the Ferrari I was driving in Italy, I was very careful to put in the right fuel type. You see, you can't put low grade fuel into a high grade car. The precision that makes them great, also requires precise care.

We're the same. In fact, people are far more precisely made than Aston Martins or Ferraris. If we put junk food, alcohol or drugs in, where good food and pure water should go, well, it's not going to end well for us, either. We're finely crafted, high precision machines – we need to take excellent care of our finely tuned machinery or, like a super car filled with kerosine, we won't like the results!

Also, the nicer the car, the more irreplaceable it is. Take for example a 1962 Ferrari 250GT Spyder. A nice version of that car sells for $15 million. Yes, you really did read that right - $15 million for one car! Can you imagine how the owner of the Ferrari 250GT in Dubai felt recently when he came back to find the valet had crashed his precious car! It's literally irreplaceable as no two are exactly the same. And of course, once wrecked, it can never be the same again.

That's also like people. Every one of us is unique and irreplaceable. Once we're gone, well, we're gone and no one else can fill the gap we leave. I know, because I had a very good friend Roger who's gone. How good of a friend was he? Roger was my roommate in boarding school. We had all sorts of crazy adventures together. I tell you all about one of them in "Disneyland's Back Door." I'd give up all the fancy cars in the world to have my friend Roger back.

Roger was irreplaceable. We all are irreplaceable. "I am irreplaceable" – go ahead and say it. It's true. Irreplaceable to your friends, irreplaceable to family, and irreplaceable to God.

I picked up a targa top Corvette Stingray at LA Airport. That car has over 500 horsepower. It's a genuine monster! But there was one little problem - LA traffic jams. You see, it doesn't matter how fast your car can go, when you're in traffic you can only go as fast as cars around you. And that's a lot like life. Who we surround ourselves with, determines how fast and how far we can go.

We are made to achieve great things. But if our friends are all dragging us down, we never reach our full potential.

So, if you meet someone, and you think they're just great. That's cool. But ask yourself this: Is this person going to help me achieve the potential God has given to me, or are they going to take me away from God's plan for my life? Make no mistake, who our friends are has a HUGE impact on the speed we'll be able to travel in life – and the direction we will go.

Don't believe me? Remember how I told you about my wife at the beginning of this story? Her name is Leisa. And she is very beautiful. She's very smart. But more than all of that, she loves God. And that has really helped me to love God. And she loves me. And that's why she sent me off on my Paris adventure – see, true love is super cool! Better even than a convertible yellow Lamborghini through the streets of Paris on a hot summer day. Though, if you get the chance, you really should try the Lambo!

Hey, to really get this story, you've got to see the photos of the Lamborghini in Paris, the Aston Martin in England, the Ferrari in Italy, the Corvette in California, a very cute bug-eyed Citroën 2CV on the French Riviera, and much more. So pop over and visit:

www.brownroadbooks.com and click on the ***Extras*** button on the top menu - the pictures from the Ferrari museum are particularly amazing!

Ice Christmas

What are the two happiest words in the English language?

Dinner's ready?

Pay day?

Kiss me?

Well, those are all happy enough if the context is right.

But in my mind, the two happiest words are "snow camp."

I know this because when I was in my last year of high school, I was invited to a snow camp, and I can't ever remember being quite as excited.

When we arrived at camp, it wasn't initially obvious what to do. During summer they water ski on the lake. They hike in the woods. They sit around campfires under the stars and tell stories. All of that. But when it's winter? Wow. I didn't want to sit around outside! And I sure wasn't jumping in the lake. After all, it was frozen over!

That's when the camp counselor said, "Why not canoe down the river?"

I have to say, I thought it was a very odd idea. Who goes canoeing in the middle of winter? But before I could say anything, Jenny piped up, "Yes, let's go. And James and Burt, you can come in my canoe."

Jenny was the most beautiful girl in the entire high school. At least that's what I thought at the time. I suppose you could say I had a crush on her. So I would have pretty much gone anywhere as long as she asked me.

"James, I'm jumping into the middle of this skunk nest," Jenny said laughing and pointing at the old silver canoe. "Are you going to get in the front, or are you just going to stand there gawking?"

Wow, Jenny, you bet, anywhere with you! I thought. But all I said was a very slow "Sure…"

Of course I was going if Jenny was going. Plus, I suspected that Burt liked Jenny, too. I wasn't about to watch Jenny paddle off with Burt leaving me looking wimpy!

But still, I did think canoeing in winter seemed strange, and so I said to the counselor, "How can you canoe during winter?"

"Oh, just like any other time of year, except you wear more clothes!" he said, chuckling.

"But what about the ice?" I didn't know very much about winter, but I knew enough to know that you can't canoe over ice!

"Don't worry, the river here has never iced over – not even in the coldest winters. You see, when water is running this fast, ice doesn't form on the top."

It all sounded a bit odd to me, but he was the counselor, so he should know, right? And besides, while I was questioning the counselor, Jenny and Burt had dragged a bright silver aluminum canoe out of the shed and were sliding it along the snow towards the banks of the river. Jenny looked back at me over her shoulder, laughed and said, "Hey James, how about a little bit of help here, big guy?"

~

I ran over, grabbed the side of the canoe and began to help push.

Of course, you have to be careful getting into a canoe from a snowy riverbank. Burt graciously said, "James, you get in up front." So I did. He pushed the canoe into the water, then Jenny jumped in the middle. Finally, Burt used his paddle to push the back of the canoe off the snow bank and into the flowing water.

Although it was cold, the sun was shining brightly. The sky was bright blue. With my big down jacket on, I was warm enough. And I have to say, at that moment I thought there was nothing better in all the world than canoeing in winter. Why would anyone canoe at any other time?

The pure white snow almost glowed in the sunshine. The beautiful trees had icicles on them where the snow had melted and refrozen. In the sunshine they looked like forests of the most beautiful Christmas trees. And once we were around the river bend from our launching site, we were completely alone. Just three kids, surrounded by the most beautiful scene you could ever imagine. We paddled smoothly and slowly. The water made a lovely lapping sound. And the canoe just glided along with the current.

We must have gone a couple of miles before the river took a sharp snaking turn to the left. No problem. We paddled on. Everything was going to plan.

"What's the favorite book you've read recently?" Jenny asked as we paddled.

I thought about it for a minute as I dug my paddle deep into the water.

"I did like *'The Hitchhikers Guide to the Galaxy,'*" I responded.

"What's that about?"

I laughed, "About hitchhiking around the galaxy of course! And a whole adventure that goes along with it - including Arthur Dent falling in love with a beautiful girl named Trillian..."

I was silent for a second as I thought of Jenny - she was even more beautiful than I'd imagined Trillian to be. And, if it weren't for Bert, well this could be our romantic moment!

After a minute in wistful wonder, we started talking again as we softly paddled along, the river's current doing most of the work. It was really nice to have Jenny asking me questions. She really seemed interested in me - or was she just bored and passing the time?

"Look over there!" Bert called pointing into the sky.

I looked in the direction of his finger. For a second I didn't see anything. And then, there, above the river was the most magnificent bird I'd ever seen. It had huge wings - with wingtip feathers that sprung out like wild finger tips. It had a pure white tail, and the most amazing white head.

"It's a bald eagle!" cried Bert.

I'd never seen anything like it. It was so powerful, graceful - it was majestic!

We were busy looking into the sky as we casually guided our silver canoe through the beautiful fresh water. When the river took a sharp turn to the left, we floated along with it. And then, when it jutted back to the right, we made the turn without too much effort.

I may have been new at this canoe business, but I was in a good team. And, I had to admit, Bert was doing a great job guiding us. He knew his way around a canoe - and skillfully told us who should be doing what and when, to make sure our progress was smooth.

I was feeling very confident when we paddled into a part of the river that was deeply shaded on both sides by high trees that hung over the bend. As we made the turn, the sun was beginning to set in the short winter afternoon. It took a moment for my eyes to adjust to the shaded river in the fading light. I blinked as I looked ahead. Was it possible? No. Maybe it was just a reflection? I peered carefully ahead. And then the words just tumbled out of my lips, "Ice ahead!"

$\sim$

Jenny looked up. And Burt strained to see past her. "What? I don't believe it! The counselor said this river never freezes," said Jenny.

Burt, who knew a lot about the outdoors, remained silent for a minute. And then, in a very low voice said slowly, "We're in trouble."

"Let's paddle back," I said optimistically.

"We can't," said Burt with a hint of irritation, "the current's too strong for us to fight and the light is fading. We'd never get back before the temperature drops to the point where we can't survive out here."

"What if we hike back?" I suggested.

"The forest is thick and we have no idea where the tracks are. The only way we could navigate is via the sun and look…" Burt pointed to the sun setting behind the trees.

I'm not given to panicking, but just then the bow of our canoe collided with the ice shelf and the screech of the hollow metal against the shattering ice sent a very literal chill down my spine.

The current pulled the canoe side on against the ice shelf and for a second I thought it might flip us over.

Just at that moment Jenny said something that seemed insane at the time, "OK, we've got no choice, guys, let's jump out and drag the canoe over the ice."

"No way," I said without thinking, "even I know you don't walk on river ice in winter!"

Burt agreed, "Jenny, we've got to think of a better idea. Let's try to smash the ice with our paddles."

All three of us began whacking the ice, and as we did, our canoe began dangerously lurching from side to side. Despite our best efforts, we couldn't crack through the ice.

"See, I told you," said Jenny, "we've got to chance it on the ice. James, you're at the front, you get out and pull us…"

I looked back at Jenny. She was smiling. My heart melted just a little. And I thought, *If I'm going to freeze to death, I may as well freeze to death happy.*

I prayed as hard as I could and then I slowly pulled myself out onto the ice. First one foot. Then the next. And then I began pulling the canoe up. Soon Jenny and Burt were out and the three of us slid the canoe across the ice like a gigantic ice ski.

It's strange how quickly something so totally crazy becomes entirely normal. The ice creaked under us. But, so far, none of it cracked open. This river not only froze – it froze thick! So much for the camp counselor's counsel...

The problem with pushing canoes across ice is that progress is slow. And bit by bit the sun was setting. "Study the ice in front of us," instructed Bert, "and be alert. It may break up at any moment and we want to be back in the canoe before that happens!"

We lugged that old canoe for what seemed like forever. Night fell on us as we were still sliding it. I wanted to give up. I really did. But what choice did we have? And by this time I was getting cold. Real cold. The kind of cold I'd never felt in my entire life. Not just in my fingers, which were numb. Or my toes. Not even just my face. But deep in my body the chill was starting to seep through.

We came around another bend in the river and, in the blue darkness, I just made out some broken ice up ahead. "Look, the ice, it's breaking up," I called.

Jenny looked carefully for a minute, "Let's keep close to the canoe and get ready to jump in if the ice cracks on us."

I did my best to follow her instructions. Then the ice beneath me cracked with an awful crack. "Get back in the canoe, big guy," she yelled. I didn't need to be told twice. I leapt in, and with it, the ice under the bow gave way. Jenny was quick to follow. But Bert kept pushing us from the back.

"Get in Bert," Jenny called.

"If I do, we won't get off the ice. I'll push just a little bit more."

"Get in!" Jenny commanded, but Bert wasn't listening.

The ice was cracking all around us.

"Bert!"

~

Just at that moment, Bert leapt in. The canoe listed side to side for a minute, and then he dug his paddle deep into the water and we were on our way.

Canoeing down the river in the darkness was, if anything, more beautiful than in the light. The stars above us sparkled in the inky black sky, the river seemed to flow even more gently, and the woods were beautifully still with just the occasional tinkling sound when a breeze moved the icicles.

"How will we know when we've arrived?" I asked innocently.

"I've been thinking that myself," said Bert. "This river winds for miles and miles. With no towns. I guess we just have to hope we bump into people somewhere."

The three of us were quiet for a minute. Until that point we'd been so busy, we didn't have time to wonder how we'd get shelter that night.

"I'm getting really cold," said Jenny. "Really cold."

"Just keep paddling," said Bert, "I'm sure we'll find someone."

But the way he said it made me think he wasn't sure at all.

It was well after dark when we came around a bend and there in front of us was the happiest sight I've ever seen.

Shooting out across the river like the beams from a double lighthouse was a 4x4's headlights on high beam.

"Hooray!" we seemed to all yell in a raggedy sort of way. We were safe!

The camp counselor was pacing next to his 4x4 as he peered out into the blackness.

When we paddled up to the bank, the first thing he said was, "Where on earth have you guys been! You've broken the world record for the slowest canoe team on earth!" His face was red, and he sounded very angry.

"No we haven't," said Jenny in a deadpan way.

"Well, you're certainly the slowest canoeists this camp has ever seen," the counselor said with a mix of relief and reproof.

"No we're not," said Jenny with a wry smile.

"Well, no one has ever taken longer than you!"

"That may be true, but that's because we only canoed half the river."

"Half? Well, then you should have made it in half the time then, shouldn't you!"

"Except that we canoe-skied the other half," said Jenny with a hint of irony. "And we are the fastest canoe-skiers this camp has ever seen!"

"What, I've never heard of such a thing!" The counselor was dumb-founded. "What kind of nutty stunt have you pulled?"

Bert began laughing and explained the entire saga. The counselor's mouth gaped open. "You kids were dragging a canoe over virgin ice? Are you crazy? What if one of you had fallen in? You would have died in a matter of minutes!"

"We didn't have much choice," Jenny explained.

The counselor just shook his head, "That's the wildest story I ever heard."

He thought about it for a minute. Screwed up his nose, and blurted out, "But this river has never iced over. Never!"

"Not quite never," I said. "We'd be happy to take you back and show you where it certainly has iced over this year. But," and at this point we were all shivering – half out of relief and half out of the bone chilling cold of the winter night, "we're a little cold."

"Yes, yes, of course, into the truck, let's get you back to the cabin."

∽

That night sitting in the cabin with Jenny on one side and Bert on the other I was very thankful.

Thankful for the crackling open fire with its rich pine smoke wafting up and out the chimney.

Thankful for the big cup of dark hot chocolate resting between my hands.

Thankful for Bert's knowledge of the woods.

Thankful for Jenny's clever leadership.

Thankful for our great friendship.

And thankful that somewhere, way up there beyond the stars there's a God who looked down on us three kids and somehow kept the ice from shattering underneath us.

When Christmas rolls around each year, I often think back on that snow camp adventure. And I wonder what would have happened had that ice cracked beneath us. I shudder to think!

You might think that with such a great adventure, this Christmas I'll take my family to a snow-camp?

No way!

You see, I like a white Christmas. But I don't like an ice-Christmas. The cold just isn't for me. So when I think about a white Christmas, it isn't white snow and ice I think of. No, I dream of something entirely different - beautiful white sandy beaches. And instead of ice on the water, I dream of white foam on top of perfect azure blue waves rolling into the beach.

This year I'll be dreaming of a white Christmas, for sure. Sitting by a beach enjoying the sunshine!

To see some photos of the beach in Sydney where I own a home, visit:

www.brownroadbooks.com and click on the *Extras* button on the top menu - maybe you'll want to come over to our home next Christmas!

Photos

Why have an ice Christmas, when you can have a nice Christmas at the beach? And sometimes we have very good company on Christmas Day!
For many more photos of James' beach, visit: www.BrownRoadBooks.com and click on "Extras"

Now that's what we call a great Christmas Day in Australia!
For many more photos of James' beach, visit: www.BrownRoadBooks.com and click on "Extras"

Or would you prefer to just sit down and relax?
For many more photos of James' beach, visit: www.BrownRoadBooks.com and click on "Extras"

Photos

Nothing feels better than driving a Lamborghini in Paris!
Do you see Napoleon's arch in the background?
For many more photos of the cars James drove,
visit: www.BrownRoadBooks.com and click on "Extras"

Just one of the Ferrari's in Modena, Italy
For many more photos of the Ferraris in Italy,
visit: www.BrownRoadBooks.com and click on "Extras"

Photos

Meeting a Malaysian monkey who looks very
much like James' pet monkey.
For another photo of Malaysian monkeys, visit: www.BrownRoadBooks.com and click on "Extras"

Crawling through the forgotten fort's tunnels isn't so scary when
they're lit and there's no terrifying mystery waiting for you!
For many more photos of the forgotten fort, visit: www.
BrownRoadBooks.com and click on "Extras"

Photos

Is this the most beautiful house in the world?
If so, where is it, and who built it?
For more photos of *the most beautiful house in the world*, visit:
www.BrownRoadBooks.com and click on "Extras"

With WWII war relics on a tiny island you've never
heard of (unless you've read "John & and the Giant Croc")
For more photos of from the island and a photo of John,
visit: www.BrownRoadBooks.com and click on "Extras"

John & the Giant Croc

Some people don't like to swim in the ocean because they're scared of sharks. Not me! I know you can count on your hand how many people are killed by sharks in a year – it's so fantastically unlikely, I just never even think about it.

But there's something I find really scary that you find in the water if you go to the right places. Or maybe I should say, the wrong places!

Piranhas?

No.

Killer whales?

Much worse than them!

Stingrays?

Not even close!

I'm talking about crocs!

I don't mean the shoes. I mean the real thing! Big, huge saltwater crocodiles. And sometimes I travel to places where there are plenty of those huge monsters.

Don't get crocs mixed up with alligators. Yes, alligators can be dangerous. But they aren't nearly as aggressive as the saltwater crocodiles that live in parts of the Pacific.

One day I flew to the tiny island of Emirau. No matter how long you live, my guess is you'll never get to Emirau because you'll need your own plane to get there. You aww, no airline flies there. And no ferry goes there. It's that remote!

Today everyone on the island is a Christian. Well, everyone except the crocodiles. More on them in a minute.

Emirau sits right near the equator which means it's hot every day of the year. And there's no air-conditioning there. Do you know the way to stay cool? Jump in the ocean, of course. So that was exactly where we headed after a long hard day.

I've been to some nice beaches. And I've seen some clear water. But I have to say this water was so clean you could see for miles! And the beaches? Pure white fine powder sand. And everywhere you look in the water are the most beautiful fish. You want my vote for the best beach in the world? I vote Emirau number one!

And it's not just the beach. There is a nice high platform that juts out over a particularly deep part of the bay. And do you know what was going on? Kids were running up the platform and diving into the water. Some were even doing somersaults before splashing down. It was terrific fun!

After we were finished snorkeling, a beautiful lady from the village brought us all something to drink.

What do you think it was?

Maybe a can of Sprite?

No way! They don't have cans of soda on the island.

They have something a whole lot better - fresh coconuts just knocked off the tree. And we sat on that beautiful beach drinking fresh, sweet coconut milk right out of the coconut. It was just so, so refreshing. There really couldn't be anything better!

After a nice swim, we went back to the village. And that's where I met John. One of his friends said to John as we talked, "Take off your shirt". I thought, *That's a strange way to start a conversation...*

～.?

When John took his shirt off, I immediately realized something pretty awful had happened to him. All over his body were the most incredible scars – it looked like he'd been attacked by a chainsaw!

"What on earth happened to you?" I blurted out, so loudly, I felt a little embarrassed.

"Let me tell you the story," replied John.

It turns out John loves to fish. And the best place to fish? Down at the mangroves. Mangroves look like bushy trees above the water, and under the water they look like webs of roots. And the mangroves are where lots of fish like to swim.

John didn't use a net or a line to fish. He used a spear. And his method was simple. Sink down into the dark waters under the mangroves and wait for big, juicy fish to swim above him. Then, just at the right moment, bam! Up flew his spear through the water, and he caught another fish.

John surfaced gasping for air after every catch, and then trod water as he tied each new fish to a string around his waist. John was having a great day fishing. He thought about grilling those fish over charcoal, adding a little coconut cream and salt to them, and eating a lovely Friday evening dinner with his family.

After he'd caught his breath, he slunk back down to the bottom of the mangroves hoping to catch just one more fish. And that's when it happened.

He felt something scratching his leg. A mangrove root or maybe a sunken tree branch?

He looked around in the murky water, and that's when his heart almost failed. There, right behind him, was an enormous salt water croc with its jaws wide open!

John instinctively kicked as he swam desperately up to reach the surface. But he wasn't quick enough. The croc grabbed onto his left leg with its mighty jaws. John kicked wildly with his right leg. Blood started pouring from the cuts in his leg. His lungs were filling with water. The surface looked a thousand miles away.

He gave the croc one more mighty kick in the nose. And, amazingly, the croc let go. But just for a second. He was almost to the surface of the water, when the mighty croc struck again, this time grasping his chest between its jaws and ripping a large chunk of skin off.

Somehow John managed to get to the beach and struggle up. But then the monster croc came lunging out of the water onto the land.

John tried to climb up a little mangrove tree, but the croc swiveled around and knocked him out with its tail.

John jumped up. He was bleeding from the deep cuts in his chest and legs. He began to run back to the water as he had nowhere else to go. And then he got the most chilling surprise.

The croc stood up on its hind legs, grabbed him with its front legs, and bam, slammed its huge jaw down on the top of John's head. John's body went limp, and he fell straight into the water. Was that it for John?

~✺

John lay in the water, looking up, and floating, knowing the croc would finish him off at any moment. And while floating he prayed the most heartbreakingly simple prayer:

"Lord, this is your servant John. When you come again, please don't forget about me lost here in the mangroves."

As he waited to die, his body drifted with the current. How long he drifted, John can't say. But long enough for him to float around the corner to a place where a waterfall plunged into the mangroves.

And just as he came under the waterfall, a strong man's voice commanded him, "Reach up!"

John couldn't believe what he was hearing. He looked around, but in his faint condition, couldn't see anyone. Desperate, John reached up his hand in hope.

And that strong arm reached down, firmly grabbed John's arm, and pulled with all his might. He then put John, ragged and bleeding, on his shoulders and ran at full speed back to the village.

When they arrived, it was obvious to the chief that John was going to die. After all, he was bleeding from cuts all over his body. And there's no hospital on Emirau. The chief ran to the two-way radio and put out a call for help. And this is where things get even weirder.

As I told you at the beginning, there are no planes that fly to Emirau. But, it just happened that, at that exact moment, the mission plane was flying right overhead on its way to another island. The pilot diverted. John was rushed onto the plane, and as quickly as possible, John was in a hospital bed on a large neighboring island.

~

When John finished his story, he said, laughing, "I don't go fishing in the mangroves anymore!"

I don't blame him.

"But I was swimming this afternoon," I said to John. "No one told me there were huge man-eating crocodiles around!"

"Were you swimming in the mangroves?"

"No, I was at the beach."

"No problem, crocs like the mangroves."

"Yeah, but the mangroves are just around the corner from the beach."

John laughed a belly laugh again and shrugged his shoulders as if to say, "You worry too much."

And maybe I do. But, when there are man-eating giant crocs in the neighborhood, I think it makes sense to worry a little, don't you?

"Whenever I think of that story, James," John continued, "I think of someone else – someone who rescues us from our powerful enemy - can you guess who?"

I've put John's answer below, but I wonder if you can come up with his answer all by yourself?

～

John was happy in the dirty mangrove water. He didn't see the danger. He'd gone there because he thought he'd get something he wanted. And at first, he believed he was doing really well. But little did he know that all the time that big old croc had his eyes on him. He had come into the croc's dirty old territory, and he was happy for John to get a few fish and think he was going to get away with it.

But with every passing minute John was getting more tired and more weak. And then, just when John was at his weakest, the croc came in for the kill. The croc almost got John. John couldn't fight him on his own.

But he didn't have to.

Instead, someone strong and filled with love reached his powerful arm down and pulled John out. And then he carried John to safety. Which made John think of someone else...

You see, that old croc reminds John of Satan. Satan has 1,000 ways to try to destroy us. And he'll do anything to hurt us. If we go into his territory, well, he'll let us feel like we're getting what we want for a while. But he's just waiting for us to get weaker and weaker. And then he goes in for the kill – just like the croc.

But then someone says, "reach up, and I'll pull you to safety." That rescuer is Jesus. Once we're in our rescuer's arms, nothing the Devil tries can hurt us. We're safe!

I'm sure thankful that someone reached down and saved John from that croc. But you know what? I'm even more thankful that Jesus came down from Heaven to save all of us forever! How about you?

To see photos of John, the most beautiful beach in the world, some of the war relics from Emirau, visit: www.brownroadbooks.com and click on the *Extras* button on the top menu - it is one of the most interesting places you'll ever see!

The Incredible Island of Emirau

No airline flies to Emirau, but there's a beautiful paved landing strip on the tiny island. Why?

For that you have to go all the way back to World War II when the Australians, New Zealanders and Americans were fighting the Imperial Japanese Army in what is now northern Papua New Guinea.

The Japanese captured a large area, but the Americans built a secret airbase on Emirau. During the entire war, it was never discovered.

The island is still full of old war materials. There are even old planes crashed out in the jungle. I went to one village, and a man brought me a huge unexploded shell from a big gun for me to see. "Do you want to come close and have a good look," he asked. My answer? "No, not really!" After all, you should never get close to explosives!

The beaches on Emirau are amazing. One of the incredible animals in the water is the "Disco Clam." Some people call it the "Electric Flame Clam" because of the bright colors that flash across the huge clam's mouth. You really have to see one to believe it!

But the best part of Emirau is the people. They are the nicest, kindest, most generous people you'll meet anywhere. And you know why? Because the love of God just shines out of their hearts! Emirau is a wonderful place - as long as you don't get mixed up with a croc while you're there!

The Forgotten Fort

"Hey kids, I think I've found something amazing," my dad's voice boomed from the living room of our home on the tropical island of Penang, Malaysia.

"What is it dad?" I asked as I ran in.

"I've found an old report that there's a large fort over looking the water on the south-western tip of our island."

"I've never heard of any fort," I said puzzled.

"That's the point," he replied, "I think it's been forgotten. I've looked at modern maps, and all the area shows is thick jungle. But look at this," he said pointing to a very old, large, leather bound book.

I looked over his shoulder, and sure enough, there was an old picture of an imposing fort and a map.

"You mean that out there in the middle of the jungle is a huge old fort?"

"It certainly looks like it," my dad replied with a hint of mystery. "Any interest in trying to rediscover it?"

Any interest, are you kidding me? I was over the moon with excitement. So were my brothers. And when we told our friends, they went almost crazy with curiosity.

Who wouldn't want to search for a forgotten fort?

"If we were going on an adventure to find a lost fort," my dad said, "we need the right gear."

That sounded exciting, what kind of gear was my dad talking about?

"First, you'll need to wear long sleeves and long pants"

That was boring, and it didn't seem like a good idea either. So, I said "I don't want to do that, dad, it's boiling hot in the jungle."

"But the jungle also has leeches, Jamie," my dad reminded me, "and if you don't want to come home with leeches hanging off you sucking your blood, you need to dress properly."

He had a point. I'd had those little squirmy slug-like things with their blood sucking mouths stuck on me before. And I sure didn't want them again!

"Second, you'll need a good hat. Third, a big water bottle - hacking your way through thick jungle is thirsty work. Fourth, you'll need a flashlight. And finally..."

At this point he called me over, reached down, and handed me something amazing.

"Finally, you'll need a machete. Now, be sure to be careful with the machete - its broad, long sword-like blade is for cutting the jungle, not cutting yourself by mistake!"

Wow, a great big machete to hack through jungle! This was going to be seriously awesome!

I was pumped to the ceiling when we set off for the jungle. We were about to find a lost fort, and uncover every bit of treasure there! Or were we?

∽

When we arrived at the edge of the jungle, my spirits began to sag. I stood looking at the wall of trees, vines, bushes and overgrowth. There was no path. And the jungle went for miles and miles.

"How on earth will we be able to find anything in there?" I gasped.

"That's the point Jamie," my dad said patiently, "it's not going to be easy. But let's give it a try!"

I was quiet after that, but in my head I thought *this is a lost cause! There's no way we'll find anything other than bugs in this wall of green!*

But, with the rest of them, I set off marching into the jungle like a line of soldiers on a doomed mission.

It was hot. Steamy. And the jungle really was full of creepy crawlies.

We'd only been hacking our way through the jungle for a few minutes when I walked face first into a banana spider's web - "Agghhh!"

Spider web was in my mouth, my eyes, wrapped around my nose and all over my hair. It was disgusting! And if there's one thing I hate, it's spiders with their little scratchy legs, their poisonous fangs, their beady strange eyes. "Urrggghr" I let out another sound as I furiously tried to clear the web off my face.

"Just hold it!" yelled my brother Steve.

"What?"

"You've got something on the back of your neck…"

At that moment I felt the worst scratchy feeling ever. Something was crawling on me. I shuddered and screamed, "No!"

"Just hold still," my dad commanded. "I'll grab it!"

But I couldn't. I was so freaked out.

Even as I squirmed, I felt my dad's big hand on the back of my neck. And in an instant the crawling stopped.

"Hmm," said my dad, "the little blighter got me!"

I turned around, and sure enough, there was an impressive red mark on my dad's finger. I should have felt bad about it. But I was so relieved to have the spider off my neck, all I felt was gratitude.

"Thanks dad, you're the best," I said in relief.

My dad laughed as he squeezed his finger, "It sure hurts a lot to be the best!"

That drama over, we soldiered on because somewhere in this mass of green, was the goal of our adventure.

At least we hoped it was.

But after an hour hacking our way through the thickest jungle you could ever imagine, no one was sure of anything. And what if we were getting hopelessly lost?

"Hey, watch out with your machete!" yelled my brother Stephen. Oops, in my enthusiasm swinging wildly at the jungle vines, I'd almost chopped into his shoulder!

"Maybe we have the wrong location," I wondered aloud. "I mean, we would have found it by now, right?"

The words were just out of my mouth when Stephen cried out "Look - here's the remains of a wall!"

～

I ran up to take a look, but when I saw it, I was disappointed. "It's just a lousy old wall. It could be anywhere. There's nothing to look at," I complained.

"Let's just follow the wall," Steve said, "and maybe it'll lead us to the rest of the fort."

"It's just a boring wall!" I repeated. "How much longer will we be hacking our way through this?" "C'mon," said Steve with determination, "we've made it this far, we can't give up now!"

Why can't we give up, I thought. We'd given up on a lot of easier things than this! But I was outvoted, so off we went, hacking our way again.

It wasn't long before we came to a couple crumbling buildings, pitch dark inside and dank with years of water damage. Jungle fungi grew all over the damp walls of the rooms. I looked in, but there didn't really seem to be much to see. An empty room. Yawn. "This isn't working out too well, is it?" I said, bored, tired and with sweat soaking through my shirt.

"We're just at the beginning," my brother Tim said, "it's a bit early to call our adventure a failure!"

After a few minutes, Steve yelled "Stop!" I was trailing behind and couldn't understand his command.

"What's going on?" I queried.

"Come and see.... but be very, very careful!"

～

I inched up cautiously and looked over his shoulder as he pointed straight down with his machete.

Right in front of us, hidden by the jungle, was a long drop of about ten feet. It looked like we'd stumbled on a huge round empty concrete swimming pool.

"Wow, that would have been painful to fall into!" I said.

"Worse than that," said Steve, "how would we ever have climbed out?"

I looked at its smooth concrete walls, and wondered who on earth would build a huge round concrete hole in the middle of the jungle.

As I was thinking about the mystery, my brother Tim called out, "There's a rusty old metal ladder over here!"

"Do you think it'll hold?" my dad asked.

Tim looked at it carefully. "Yeah, I think so. But probably only for kids." And with that, he stepped onto it. We watched he climbed carefully down.

Once at the bottom he called up, "You've got to come and see what I've found down here." I didn't need a second invite. Finally - something worth looking at! As soon as I got to the concrete floor, I followed Tim around the edge. And there it was - a door.

By this time, my oldest bother had joined us. "Should we go in?" Steve asked.

"Well..." I said hesitating.

It was pitch black inside the room, and my eyes were adjusting from the bright sunlight. "Who knows what was in there?" I worried.

In truth, it didn't look inviting at all.

"Let's take a look around first," I said, buying some time.

We walked around the edge of the concrete hole. "I'm still puzzled by what this place is," Steve said.

"Maybe looking in the room will help us figure it out," I wondered aloud, regretting the words as soon as I uttered them.

"Yeah, great idea," said Steve as he motioned me back to the mysterious door.

~

As I peered into the darkness behind the doorway, Steve called to me "Turn on your flashlight."

Of course, that's what I needed to do! I shone the beam of light in, and was instantly glad I did. The door didn't go into a room as I imagined, but rather it was the opening to a deep shaft straight down. "Wow, I'm sure glad I didn't try to walk in!" I exclaimed.

I shone the beam upwards, where it rested on a strange metal-looking machine like nothing I'd ever seen. When I shone the light down again, I noticed there was a metal ladder down one side. I leaned in and shone the light straight down. Wow, the shaft was deep. Really deep!

"Let's go take a look," Steve said. "You're the smallest, Jamie, why don't you go first."

I gulped. *Why me?* But still, someone had to go. And I didn't want to look chicken. So I cautiously put my foot on the first step on the ladder.

My dad called down from above the rim, "Be careful there, boys."

"Don't worry dad," Steve called back, "it's all under control."

Really? I thought as I climbed down cautiously, *it doesn't feel very controlled!*

The small metal steps were slippery, and the narrow shaft walls seemed very close on every side. I couldn't hold my flashlight while I climbed down, so I just bucked up, and climbed into the complete darkness.

When I arrived at the bottom of the ladder, I looked up. The door, with its narrow beam of light, looked miles away. I gulped. What if we got trapped down here?

I didn't have much time to think about it as there was something else that caught my attention...

As I tuned my flashlight back on, I immediately saw something intriguing. "Hey, there's a tunnel that goes off from both sides down here," I called up.

I crawled into the small tunnel - the beam from my flashlight showed nothing but the four perfectly formed concrete walls of the narrow tunnel, which gently curved like it was part of a huge circle that mirrored the curve of the big hole far above it.

Steve and Tim climbed down behind me. And as each arrived at the bottom of the shaft, they had to crawl into the tunnel to make way for the next person. I was being pushed deeper and deeper into the tunnel - and further and further from escape.

The air felt stale. The space was very tight. And, as I crawled along the curving tunnel, I soon realized I could no longer see the opening to the tunnel behind me.

All of a sudden, I became very afraid. Here I was far under the earth in a tiny tunnel, crawling along, with no idea what was ahead. No idea at all...

I proceeded ever so cautiously.

"Hurry up, Jamie," called Steve, "let's see what's in here!"

I didn't care what he said, I was going slow. After all, anything, literally anything, could be up ahead. A huge drop, a wild animal, a trap. Anything!

And then it happened.

I turned the corner.

There it was!

All the way down here in this tiny tunnel.

I blinked for a second not believing what I was seeing.

There, right in front of me, a wild looking skull was staring right back at me!

I let out a scream!

And everyone else yelled too!

"What is it?" cried Steve.

"It's a skull!" I shouted.

"What?" screamed my brothers in unison.

My heart was pumping so hard, I could hardly think. I wanted to jump up and ran away. But I couldn't even stand because the concrete ceiling was so low. And I couldn't go to the left - the wall was so close, my elbow scraped on it. And I couldn't move to my right. And I couldn't go back because my brothers blocked the path behind me.

"Go back, go back, go back!" I screamed in a complete panic, "I gotta get out of this place!"

But my brothers weren't going back, instead they were pushing me forward - they were full of curiosity.

"What kind of skull?" Steve pressed me.

Up until that point, I hadn't really thought about it. I tried to calm myself, and slowly pointed my flashlight forward again through the pitch blackness.

As the beam followed the floor, it revealed big incisor teeth. A long snout. And big empty eye sockets.

On second inspection, it certainly wasn't a human skull. Steve looked over my shoulder.

"Looks like a dog's skull," he said after a minute. "And look, his whole skeleton is down here."

"How on earth would a dog be down here?" I wondered aloud.

"Poor fellow," Steve mused, "must have somehow fallen down the shaft and, with no way to get out, he must have died down here."

That was all I needed to hear. "I've got to get out of here, guys," I said. "I don't want my skeleton to be the next one left rotting in this tunnel! One skull in the pitch darkness is enough for me!"

We shuffled backward slowly. As soon as we got to the ladder, I scampered up as fast as I could.

As I stepped back out the door, I was just so happy to be in the fresh air again!

My dad was peering over the edge, "Did I hear yelling down there - is everyone ok?"

"Yeah, we're all ok, but I'm done with crawling around tunnels, that's for sure!"

When everyone reappeared, we tried to make sense of the place.

~

Who would build a huge cement hole, and then a deep shaft down to tunnels too small for even kids to stand up in? And why would they do it?

"Come over here," said Tim. In the middle he'd found a huge rusting metal base. "Looks like the base of a gun emplacement," he said. "Must have been a huge one."

"Why put a gun in a huge concrete hole?" I queried.

"Well," began Tim who was always good with an explanation, "this sunken hole must have been where a huge cannon sat - pointing right out over the water below, defending the entire area from an attack from the sea."

"But why put it in a hole?" I pressed.

"It's good defense. Soldiers like to sink their defensive positions, because that makes them very hard to hit from below." When Tim explained it, it made sense.

"But what about the shaft and the little tunnel? What on earth could that be for?" I pondered. "I mean, who would make a tunnel so small even a kid can't stand up in it?"

"My guess," continued Tim, "is that they kept ammunition for the big gun down there."

"Why would they do that?"

"Well, the worst thing you can have happen when you've got a big gun like this, is to have your enemy hit the ammunition dump."

"Wouldn't it be worse if they hit the gun?"

"Nope. If you hit the gun, you knock out just that one gun. But if you hit the ammunition store? Well, then there's a chain reaction. One shell explodes, and that sets off the ones next to it, and so on, and then, kaboom, they all go up in one huge explosion! You can kiss your fort goodbye! So it's smart to bury the ammo deep underground to keep it safe from enemy fire."

"Hmm," I replied, "makes sense when you think about it. And that explains the mystery of why the tunnel is so small - it's not for people at all, it's for cannon shells! But what about that odd device at the top of the shaft?"

We walked over to take another look. I shone the flashlight beam up at the roof.

"Looks to me," said Tim, "it's some kind of pulley device used to get the cannon shells up quickly. It really is an impressive piece of military engineering."

It certainly was. But that left one final mystery. Why was the fort abandoned?

$\sim$

When we got home, I said to my dad, "I bet, whoever made the fort must have been safe there!"

My dad chuckled, "Well, not quite. I've found a little more information about the fort, and I think you'll find it surprising..."

"What do you mean? How could anyone conquer a fort with such huge guns - and so cleverly planned?"

"Let me tell you the story," he said. "The British built the fort when our island was part of their colonies before World War II. And, you're right, they put in all the right equipment. And not just here. All along the coast of Malaysia and Singapore, they were ready for any navy that tried to invade. After all, how could any navy survive barrages from their huge guns pointed out to sea."

"That's right," I said.

"But the British got one little thing wrong."

"What?"

"The Japanese army didn't come from the sea."

"But, but, but they must have?" I stammered, "Japan is a group of islands. They'd have no choice but to come from the sea!"

"That's what the British thought. But instead of sending their navy to Malaysia and Singapore, where they knew the British were waiting for them with their huge guns, the Japanese landed in a remote area of Thailand. You see, Thailand, Malaysia and Singapore are all connected. All the Japanese Imperial Army had to do was move down peninsula. But no one thought they could do that. After all, how can you move a huge army quickly through little roads and thick jungle?"

"You can't!" I exclaimed.

"But," my dad said with a twinkle in his eyes, "they had a secret weapon."

"Ooh," I said, trying to imagine some kind of battle-winning super gun, "what kind of secret weapon?"

"The bicycle," my dad laughed. "Believe it or not, instead of arriving on huge battleships with booming guns, the Imperial Army arrived on little bikes over land. And all the impressive British guns and their brilliantly engineered defenses? They were completely useless because the guns were all designed to shoot at big battle ships - so they pointed out to the deep sea where battle ships would have to sail - not the shallow water where little boats could take the soldiers and their bikes!"

"So bicycles beat the big British guns and massive fortifications?"

"Yes, that's about it," my dad said. "And I think there's something we can learn from that..."

~

I've thought about that story a lot since. Wars aren't always won by the side with the biggest guns or most impressive forts; they're won by the side who knows how to use the resources they have to their best strategic advantage.

It's really similar, I suppose, to the spiritual wars we fight. We can have all the resources we want. Our church might have all kinds of assets - money, hospitals, schools, real estate - all of that and much more. We may even have influence over our government. But none of those things win spiritual wars.

And if we think we're strong because of all those things, we'll be just like the British. Sitting in our forts, confident that no one can touch us. But the more confident we are, the more easily we're defeated. The devil knows our weakest point, and that's where he'll attack. Just where we're not expecting.

Is there a way to defend against our enemies more effectively than the British did? There is. But it's not through building fixed forts and hiding in them. The Bible puts it this way: its not by might or power that we achieve spiritual victory, but by the Spirit of God (Zechariah 4:6). Only God's Spirit in our hearts gives us 360 degree protection no matter what the devil tries!

~

It's been many years since we hiked into that dense jungle and stumbled on the forgotten fort with all its mysteries. Recently, the old forgotten fort was turned into a museum. I know this, because I took my girls to visit my old island home, and while there, we visited the forgotten fort.

It looks very different now! The jungle has been cleared. There are nice safe paths. And remember that deep shaft? They have a fence in front of it saying "Danger, keep out!" Which made me laugh, because little do they know that all those years ago we scampered down there with no one to tell us what to do!

In another part of the fort is an ammunition tunnel very similar to the one I crawled into all those years ago. Except that they now have museum lighting inside of it. I couldn't resist crawling into it with my youngest daughter.

As I crawled around do you know what I was thinking? "Oh, I hope there're no skulls in here!" I told my daughter, and she just laughed. But then again, its easy to laugh in a well-lit tunnel that's all clean and tidy. I'm quite sure that if she'd been with me down in the tunnel all those years ago, she'd have yelled just as loud as I did.

What do you think?

To see photos of the forgotten fort visit:

www.brownroadbooks.com and click on the ***Extras*** button on the top menu - try to imagine what the fort looked like all those years ago when it was buried under jungle!

The Imperial Officer

The first thing all the kids asked when they came to visit our home was: "What's that strange symbol on your gatepost?"

It certainly wasn't the kind of symbol you'd expect outside a doctor's home. Or a missionary's home. In fact, it wasn't something you'd expect to see outside any home at all. It looked like a very strange, very angry eagle.

And that's because it was something left over from a very grisly period of history.

You see, during the Second World War, our island was invaded by the Imperial Japanese Army. The Japanese government at the time believed they were better than all the other people in Asia. And therefore it was their right to invade all their neighbors and rule them.

Of course, when you think you're better than other people, that doesn't make you kind. In fact, those years of imperial occupation are remembered on the island as "the reign of terror."

What does "the reign of terror" have to do with our home?

Because that symbol on the gate? It was a symbol of an Imperial Army Officer.

Why was it on our home? Because during the reign of terror, a high ranking imperial officer lived right in our home! I sometimes imagine what he was like...

～

I imagine the Imperial Japanese officer standing at the door of our home, looking out over the land he'd conquered.

I imagine his hands on his hips. His puffed-out green riding trousers tucked into his knee-high jet-black leather boots. He has a straight green jacket. A row of medal ribbons sit proudly above his right pocket. And on his head is an officer's hat with one gold star in the center.

But it's what's at his side that is most eye-catching of all: a long, beautifully crafted, samurai sword. But don't be fooled by the beauty; those swords caused so much heartache on our island.

He may have believed it was his destiny to rule all of Asia forever. But it didn't work out that way. In fact, the Imperial Army's occupation lasted less than four years from the time of Japan's stunning victory, to their complete and total surrender.

I wonder if the officer who marched through our home all those years before survived the war. If he did, I wonder what he thought when the Japanese Emperor, who was supposed to be a living god, was forced to admit after surrender that he was just a guy; a guy whose army had hurt so many good people.

I wonder if the officer just went home and tried to forget everything he did and saw on our island? Did he feel guilt for what he did? Did he ever ask forgiveness? I don't know. But I hope so. I'd like to meet him in Heaven and hear all his stories. Wouldn't you?

Charlie & the Chili Challenge

My friend Charlie was a bit of a bully. I know that sounds unkind to admit, but it's true. He wasn't the worst sort of bully. He wasn't really mean. He just loved to tease. He'd tease. And then tease. And then tease some more.

I don't think he wanted to hurt anyone. He wasn't that kind of person. But he just didn't know when to stop. And sometimes not stopping when someone is clearly uncomfortable, well that's not good at all. When you don't stop with a particular kid, even after he asks you to stop, well, that crosses the line into bullying, don't you think?

One of the boys Charlie loved to tease was Juan. Juan was one of my friends, too. And sometimes he'd say to me, "Get Charlie to knock off the teasing, would you?" And I'd say, "I've tried, Juan, I really have. But it's like he's got a teasing compulsion or something. Once he starts, he can't seem to stop. In fact, the more irritated you are, the more funny he finds it, so the more he does it. It's a tragic cycle!"

"Well, one day he's going to find out the hard way that I'm tired of his teasing," said Juan. And to be honest, I believed him because Juan was a pretty strong guy. And I'd hate to think what he could do to Charlie if he wanted to. But fortunately, Juan wasn't just strong in the arms. He was strong in the brain, too. And that meant he had good self-control. Which is, I think, the most impressive kind of strength you can have. Do you agree?

Other than Charlie's teasing, there was just one other thing about our boarding school that Juan didn't like: the food.

"The food here is absolutely the worst food I've ever tasted," he told me one day. Which was odd, because I thought the food was actually quite good.

"What do you mean, Juan?" I asked.

"I mean they serve us stuff with no flavor at all. It's like eating big lumps of nothing!"

I looked at the food on my plate, and then back at Juan, and then back to my plate. Did Juan know something I didn't? The food looked - and tasted - perfectly good to me. Was there something wrong with me?

~

A few weeks later, Juan returned from home leave, and told me the most extraordinary conversation he'd had with his mother.

"Mom, they feed us the most awful food at that school," he told her.

His mom was quite surprised. "Really, Juan," she said, "how bad could it possibly be?"

"Oh, mom, it's much worse than anything you can imagine."

His mom was confused. "What's so bad about it?"

"Well, for example, they take a bunch of potatoes, boil them up and then mash them."

"Ah ha," she said, "and then what do they do with them?"

"That's the point," said Juan, "they don't do anything to them! They just slap those mashed up potatoes on a plate and you're meant to eat them!"

"Really? Just plain squished up potatoes? Nothing on them?" Mom was a little shocked herself. She was paying good money to send Juan to boarding school and they were serving him squashed up potatoes and calling it a meal?

"And it gets worse!" Charlie continued.

"Worse than that?" his mom replied.

"Yes! They boil these white noodles. Mix in some bland yellowish cheese."

"Uh hah, and then what do they do?"

"That's my point, mom, they do nothing! They just serve it to us just like that in big gooey cream colored blobs."

"Oh, Juan," said his mom, "I'm so, so sorry to hear this. Why don't you add some chili to them, at least that would give some flavor."

"I gladly would," Juan replied, "but they don't even have chilies! All they have is boring salt to go on the boring food. Look at me, mom," said Juan pointing at his stomach, "I'm getting skinny. If this goes on much longer, I'll completely waste away!"

"Oh no you won't!" laughed his mom, "I've got a plan. Follow me."

Juan followed his mom out into the garden, where his mom grew her chili plants. "Let's pick a bag full of these little fire crackers," she said, "and when you get back to school you'll at least have something to give a little taste to the 'food!'"

Together they carefully filled the clear plastic bag full of the little green chilies growing in the garden. When Juan returned to school, he was happy that, even though the food was tasteless, at least he had the necessary ingredient to add a little sparkle to it!

～

"Look what I brought from home," Juan said to me happily as he walked into the dorm holding up the little bag.

"Wow, those little green chilies look fiery hot!" I said, admiringly.

Just at that moment, who should walk by but Charlie. And the first thing Charlie noticed was the little bag of chilies.

"Hey Juan, what ya got there?" demanded Charlie.

"Chilies from my momma's garden," replied Juan with obvious pride.

"They're little bitty baby chilies!" said Charlie in a baby voice.

"No they're not!" replied Juan, clearly very irritated.

Juan's irritation delighted Charlie, who pushed on, "Little baby chillies for a little baby chicken."

Juan looked at Charlie, and for a second I was afraid he was about to clobber Charlie!

But Charlie just charged on, flapping his arms and dancing around Juan while he clucked and laughed. "Chicken chillies, chicken chillies, chicken chillies!" he repeated in the most irritatingly high baby voice he could muster.

"They're powerful chilies!" replied Juan, whose arm muscles were flexed.

Charlie, who just never knew when to stop, started to giggle. "And looky, look, your chilies aren't red hot grown up chilies, they're little chicken-boy cool green chilies. Can't handle the big red ones, eh?"

"These are plenty hot, Charlie," Juan said through clenched teeth, "trust me I know about chilies!"

Charlie started giggling even more. "Juan likes the little baby chicken-chilies not the big red hotty grown up ones," he continued in the most irritating baby voice I'd ever heard.

Juan had good self control, but I could tell he was about to explode. But somewhere in that clever brain, an idea emerged.

"You're right Charlie," he said as calmly as he could, "these are just little ones. And they're green, not red. So how hot could they possibly be?"

Charlie was grinning ear to ear with the silliest grin you've ever seen.

"So, because you know so much, how about this," Juan continued, now switching to a baby talk voice that copied Charlie. "I'll make a deal with big man Charlie. If you can keep just one of these 'little bitty baby chilies' in your mouth for just one itty bitty little minute, I'll give you ten very big boy dollars. But if you can't. Well, then you have to give me ten big boy dollars. How about that?"

Now, I grew up in Asia and I know a little about chilies. So I quickly turned to Charlie and said, "Don't do it Charlie!"

"Why not, James? Look at them! They're tiny. And they're not even red!" said Charlie with delight. He couldn't wait to pocket Juan's $10.

"But Charlie, don't you know that sometimes the hottest chilies of all, are small? And sometimes the green ones are hotter than the red ones!"

"No way!" said Charlie confidently.

I looked at him in disbelief. Charlie had never traveled anywhere. He didn't know the first thing about chilies. But he wasn't going to listen to me, I could see that in his eyes.

He turned his attention back to Juan, "You're on, my friend. Hit me with the chili of your choice, and in a minute, you'll be giving me ten big beautiful dollars!"

Now it was Juan who was giggling with delight. He put his hand carefully into the little plastic bag jammed with chilies, picked out one of the smallest and carefully handed it over to Charlie.

By this time, a large group of boys had gathered around to see what was going on.

Charlie held up the little chili so that everyone could see. All the boys were laughing. Like Charlie, they all came from homes where no one ate chilies. So they assumed that Charlie was right – a tiny green chili surely couldn't be all that hot!

And then Charlie made his huge mistake. He held his arm out straight in front of him. Opened his rather big mouth wide. And with a little flourish he popped the chili in his mouth.

"Now, you gotta chew it, but you can't swallow it," instructed Juan.

Charlie smiled and began chewing vigorously. He wanted all the other boys to see how silly Juan's little green baby chilies were - and how clever Charlie was.

But something strange happened.

First, Charlie's confident smirk began to vanish.

Then his face began turning from its pale white to an odd pink.

His eyes started bulging.

He ears even seemed to move back as his eyebrows shot up.

And that's when he started to make some very curious noises.

He started slapping the side of his leg while letting out a low groan interrupted by whistle sounds. He sounded like a broken steam train!

Instead of breathing, he started snorting through his nose.

A sort of high pitched wheeze began coming from somewhere. I looked around. No, it wasn't from someone else - it was Charlie!

His cheeks puffed out.

He then began letting out an odd whimpering sound.

I looked at my watch, "12 seconds gone, Charlie, only 48 seconds to go…"

Charlie's arm shot out and he grabbed my shoulder. And then he began shaking. His snorting became louder and louder, and then it stopped altogether. Then an amazing thing happened - something I've never seen before or since.

Charlie opened his mouth, and it was like a fountain had been turned on. Saliva shot everywhere as the boys screamed and ran to get out of the way.

I looked at my watch, "C'mon, Charlie, 21 seconds gone, only 39 to..."

But I didn't get to finish my thought because Charlie had dashed down the hallway as fast as he could to the drinking fountain and was hunched over the spout shooting cold water straight into his mouth and making a very new kind of sound something like "gwwwwakkeapphhoomethump!"

It seemed like forever, but I suppose it couldn't have been more than a few minutes, before Charlie spoke. And when he did, all he could say was "Hot, hot, ho-o-o-o-tt!"

All the boys had been laughing at Juan's chicken-boy chillies. But now, guess who they were laughing at? Poor purple-faced Charlie. And to add insult to injury, when eventually Charlie got back to normal – which I assure you was much longer than you could ever imagine – Charlie had to take the long walk down to his room, and do something he hated more than anything.

You see, Charlie loved money. So the thought of having to give ten whole dollars? Ouch, that was terrible! He rumbled through his savings, found ten crinkled old $1 bills, and then walked back to Juan.

Juan was positively gleaming as Charlie handed over his debt, one crinkly old dollar at a time. And when he'd finished paying up, Charlie said, "I guess they're not chicken-boy chillies after all..."

Charlie, who's face was still bright red, turned to me and said, "Wow, that was painful - and expensive too!"

It sure was!

And then he said the saddest words in the English language: "I've sure learned my lesson." I say those are the saddest words, as we only seem to say them after we've learned a lesson the hard way.

～

You see, there are two ways to learn things in life.

There's Charlie's method - the "hard way": Don't listen to anyone, don't observe the world around you, don't think from cause to effect. Just act like you're the first person to ever live, and life is a complete random mystery. And, then, after you get hurt, say, "I've really learned my lesson..." The problem is, sometimes the lesson is so painful, that it can mess up everything in your life and the life of people who love you. And by the time you've learned it? It's too late.

There's a second way to learn lessons - the "smart way": And it is a much smarter way. It's a way Charlie could have chosen. There's lots of things Charlie knew more about than I did, but when it came to chilies? I grew up in Asia, I've been eating chilies since I was a little kid and I love them. And Charlie knew that. Charlie knew one other thing too; I was his loyal friend. A little listening would have saved a whole lot of pain!

There are much more important lessons in life than the chili challenge. And we all have to decide how we're going to learn them. The hard way? Or the smart way?

For me, the answer is obvious. That's because I know Someone smarter than anyone else ever. And, that same Person loves me more deeply than anyone ever has. And so, when I have a big question in my life, I go to Him. And you know what I've found? I've learned so many lessons listening to God. And those lessons have brought me happiness and everything I have.

And at my house, "everything I have" always includes plenty of chilis. Because, Juan was right, just a little bit of chili makes everything taste so much better!

To read a story about my favorite curry, visit:

www.brownroadbooks.com and click on the *Extras* button on the top menu - I think you'll be very surprised at where it comes from!

Franz's Famous Flying Machine

Franz Reichelt was a French tailor with a big idea. He made himself a flying suit and decided to test it out. But how to test it? Franz came up with a "brilliant" idea. He'd climb up the Eiffel Tower in Paris, leap off, and fly over the city.

When he told people, everyone said, "Don't test it that way Franz! Put a dummy in the suit and see if it works before YOU get in the suit and jump!"

"I already put a dummy in it," replied Franz, "and it didn't work. I think it's because I didn't drop it from high enough."

"It didn't work, but now you're going to get into the suit yourself and jump from much higher?"

"Oui, that's my perfect plan," replied Franz.

"Remember all the people who have died testing crazy flying ideas," Franz friends told him. "Be smart and test your technology step by step in the safest way. Once you've proven it works, then go up to the top of the tower…"

But Franz wasn't interested in learning the smart way! He was determined to learn his lessons the hardest way possible.

Well, I don't want to tell you how that story ended, but let me just say Franz didn't get the chance to try his stunt again!

Of course, it takes courage to try things that have never been done before. That's how we get progress. But testing new ideas, and doing foolish things, are not the same thing. In fact, we need to be very wise and meticulously careful when we're testing something new. Why? Because we want to learn the smart way. Not the hard way. Ask Franz about that!

The Most Beautiful House in the World

This story is about the most beautiful house in the world. I know what you're thinking. How can anyone say which is the most beautiful house in the world? But I'll go even further! It's not only the most beautiful house, it's in the most beautiful region, of the most beautiful country on earth.

Do you know which house it is?

Well, let's work our way back to find the answer.

People like to visit beautiful places, right? So a good way to tell which is the most beautiful country on earth, is to see which country gets the most visitors. Agree?

Do you know which country gets the most visitors?

I'll give you a few hints.

Its flag is red, white, and blue.

Know yet?

OK, another clue.

Its army and navy combined to defeat the British at the battle of Yorktown.

Now can you guess?

OK, one more clue, it's where Disneyland is!

Now I know you know!

Or do you?

You see the country isn't the great United States.

No - it's France!

Didn't you know that France has a Disneyland? Well, it certainly does!

And yes, the French army and navy fought in the American Revolutionary War. France not only fought, it supplied 90% of the gunpowder used by the Americans. Without France? There'd simply be no USA!

And of course, you know the good ol' red, white, and blue is the French flag don't you?

France actually gets more tourists every year than any other nation on earth. There are about 66 million French. But every year, 84 million people come to France to visit. That's right - more people visit France than live there!

But where is the most beautiful region in France?

To answer that question, you just have to look where the old kings of France built their grandest holiday home. After all, when you're king, you can build anywhere at all - so you choose the best parts, right? And where did they choose? A little south of Paris on a beautiful windy part of the Seine River. It has lovely forests. Lots of wildlife. Everything is verdant. When you go there, it feels like you've dropped into the Garden of Eden.

There the kings built a spectacular palace named Fontainebleau. It's not the most beautiful house in the world, mind you. But it sure isn't shabby!

The first French King to live at Fontainebleau, was King Louis the Fat. Yes, that's really what they called poor old Louis VI of France. I suppose people weren't quite as polite back when they gave him that nickname!

But even if you agree that France might be the most beautiful country, and even if you go so far as agreeing with me that the region south of Paris is France's most beautiful area, how can we possibly find the most beautiful house in that region?

For that, we need a story.

A story that all begins with a guy named Nicolas Fouquet.

～

Nic was a dashing man, with long flowing dark hair and a perfectly trimmed thin mustache. He always dressed in the most expensive and elaborate clothes of his day, with large fancy collars, lots of lace and big high boots. It's hard to think of men dressing like that, but in the 1600's when Nic lived, that was all the fashion.

Nic lived during the reign of King Louis XIV - who called himself "the Sun King." And why not? When you're king, you get to say silly things like that and people have no choice but to take you seriously! The Three Musketeers story occurred around the same time as Nic lived, and that's important - as you'll see a little later.

Nic was so smart, so dashing, and so charming that the King made him head of all the King's money

That was a very high ranking job, because King Louis XIV really knew how to spend money quickly! So Nic had to run around figuring out how to get more money into the royal treasury as fast as Louis was spending it!

Fortunately for King Louis, Nic was a master at getting his hands on other people's money!

But Nic's real passion wasn't politics. Or raising money. His real passion was building his own house.

You see, Nic had land in the most beautiful region of the most beautiful country on earth, and he decided to build the most beautiful house on it.

To do that, he got the best architects. The best builders and stone masons. The best landscape gardeners and designers. And off they went to work.

No matter what they thought they should do, Nic always seemed to have the money to do it. It was amazing!

What he built was astonishing. It was big, beautiful and gorgeous in every detail. The crowning jewel of the mansion? The magnificent ballroom that is three stories high, made with white marble and a perfect dome ceiling painted like the sky. Nic called his masterpiece Vaux-le-Vicomte.

You might be imagining Nic with his dark flowing hair and fancy clothes floating around the dance floor with his wife to the sound of an elegant orchestra.

But that's what makes this story so interesting. You see, the man with the most beautiful house in the world never got to enjoy it. And there's a reason why...

When the home was finished he invited everyone who was anyone to the home for a party. And what a party it was!

King Louis? Yep, he was there in all his finery.

What about government leaders, the greatest artists, the best actors? Yes, all of them, too.

In fact, France's greatest actors performed a special play for the occasion right there at Nic's mansion.

At the end of the celebration there were even fireworks.

Nic was rich. He was powerful. And now he had the most beautiful home in France! His chest almost exploded in pride!

But all was not well.

~

King Louis heard rumors that Nic was crooked. Sure, Nic raised a lot of money for the royal treasury, but word on the street was Nic took a good chunk of change for himself!

Looking at the magnificent home, the grandest gardens in France, the fabulous party - all of it - confirmed in Louis's mind that the rumors about Nic's dishonesty were true!

And there was another thing bothering Louis.

Louis looked at Nic's house and it didn't please him at all. After all, Louis was supposed to be the "Sun King," right? He believed he should shine the brightest in his kingdom. But here was his finance man with a more beautiful house even than the king himself. And that made King Louis jealous. Super jealous. And you know one thing you never want to do? Make the king jealous!

Soon after the party, poor old Nic was arrested and thrown into a dungeon.

Who arrested Nic? It was none other than the captain of the King's Musketeers, d'Artagnan. You might recognize his name, because he's one of the famous *Three Musketeers*. Of course, the *Three Musketeers* is fiction, but it's based on real characters. And Charles de Batz-Castelmore d'Artagnan? He was a real musketeer and yes, he really did have that crazy long name, and yes, he really did arrest Nic.

So the man with the most beautiful house in the world? He never got to enjoy it. In fact, the house turned out to be his undoing.

Alexander Dumas, who wrote *The Three Musketeers*, included Nic in another of his famous books *The Man in the Iron Mask*. It is a great story. But reality wasn't too good for Nic.

Poor old Nic died in a stinky dungeon.

Everything was going so well for Nic. His family motto was, "See how high he will climb." And Nic? He'd climbed to the very top. He'd even built a house more beautiful than the king's! He was just so proud of himself.

But he fell even faster than he climbed.

Voltaire, the very famous French writer, put it this way: "At six in the evening [Nic] was the King of France: at two in the morning, he was nobody."

Nic's pride proved his undoing. And just as Proverbs 16:18 says, his pride really did go before the most amazing fall.

But the problem of pride didn't end with Nic in the dungeon. It was about to infect Louis himself and poison everything about him.

～

Louis left Nic's party with one thing in mind - he had to build a better house than Nic.

So he got Nic's brilliant team of designers and artisans and put them together with his own and instructed them to create something bigger, brighter, brasher than Nic could ever have even imagined.

His new project? The Palace of Versailles. Have you heard of that palace? It's a very famous place. And for good reason.

The White House is big, right? An average American house has around 2,000 square feet of floor space. The White House? It's got 55,000 square feet of floor space. That's almost 28 times larger than the average American home!

But if you think that's a big house, just imagine how huge the Palace of Versailles is - it's got 721,182 square feet of floor space! Versailles is 1300% bigger than the White House!

And the gardens are immense. Even now, after much of the land has been taken back and used for other things, the Palace of Versailles sits on land that is 117 times bigger than the White House grounds.

Versailles is not only massive, but it's ridiculously elaborate. I've been in the White House, which really is very fancy. But Versailles? Well, let's just say it makes the White House seem quite ordinary by comparison.

At this point, you might be thinking, *good on King Louis, he really showed Nic who's the boss, didn't he!* I suppose he did. But I don't think it did anything for Louis's soul. If you look at paintings of him around that time, he looks like an arrogant, self-centered, out-of-shape, grumpy old guy. And that's how historians describe him as well.

Yes, Louis had all the riches in the world. Yes, he built the craziest most elaborate palace you could ever imagine. And, yes Louis was so powerful he could lock Nic up and throw away the key.

But all the time, his own pride was sowing the seeds for the destruction of his kingdom.

You see, Louis didn't care much for his people who were paying all his taxes. He just spent like crazy on himself and his wars. Then he demanded even more money to spend. Well, you don't have to be an expert to know that isn't going to make people happy. He also began persecuting French Protestants who were some of the most skilled business people and bankers - so they fled the country.

Losing some of his best businesses, his smartest bankers and skilled workers wasn't a good plan. Particularly when Louis was spending money like no one ever had, on an over the top palace he didn't even need!

Louis XIV died, but the country he left was in a financial mess. The French weren't too creative when it came to the names of their kings, so the next king was Louis XV. He persecuted the Protestants and raised taxes just like Louis XIV. With similar results. He was followed by Louis XVI. And that's when the whole system came crumbling down.

The king wanted more money. The people didn't want to pay a penny more for the king's outrageously expensive way of life. The queen, Marie Antoinette, wanted to keep all the luxuries of palace life. And all the lords and ladies were far away from Paris - living in a fantasy world at the Palace of Versailles.

Well, you know how the story ended for King Louis XVI and his wife, Queen Marie Antoinette, don't you? I mention what happened to them, and where, in the "Lamborghini in Paris" story in this book. Let's just say, they really lost their heads.

Why?

In part, because Louis XIV's pride made him want a palace much bigger, grander and more impressive than Nic's magnificent home. When that crazy big palace was built, it required lots of tax money. And it moved the king out into the countryside, away from his people. Together, those things created a catastrophe for the kings of France. Nic's pride had prompted Louis' pride to grow, and Louis's pride? It destroyed everything he cared about.

~

Pride isn't just a thing that destroyed Nic and Louis. I think we're all tempted by pride. Well, at least I am. But maybe our temptations are a little different than the temptations Nic and Louis experienced?

Today there's always someone who thinks that God is wrong, and they are right. I hear it all the time. On TV, on radio, in the press. I heard it at university when I went there, and I've read it in many books. Wherever I look, people think they know better than God. That has to be the most prideful thing anyone could think - don't you agree?

We know God is all powerful and all knowledgeable. He made us. He made the entire universe. We don't even begin to compare to His understanding, that's for sure! If we want to be knowledgeable, we have to go to the source of true knowledge - God. The Bible puts it this way, "respect for God is the beginning of wisdom." But that means we have to humble ourselves first. And some people just refuse to do that. They'd rather be wrong in their pride, than right in humility. Not smart, is it.

And you know what I've found? When people get puffed up with their own pride, do you know how that ends? I'll give you a hint: think of Nic and Louis!

Pride ends in disaster, but humility ends in Heaven, where, Jesus tells us, He's prepared mansions for us. And I have a hunch - those mansions will be much nicer than Nic's "most beautiful house in the world." So much nicer that we'll look back on all the great houses and palaces in our world and shake our heads. Versailles and Vaux-le-Vicomte will look like lumps of coal, compared to what God has for us!

Would you like to see photos of "the most beautiful house in the world?" Visit:

www.brownroadbooks.com and click on the **Extras** button on the top menu - and imagine you are the lord or lady of the magnificent estate!

Louis & the Protestants

Louis XIV hated the French Protestant Christians. Remember the palace at Fontainebleau built by Louis the Fat? That is where King Louis XIV went to sign a decree outlawing Protestant Christians from practicing their faith in France. Soon French Protestants were fleeing all over the world. Some ended up in Canada. Others in America. Still others went so far as South Africa! And many went to England. Which made Louis happy - he didn't like Protestant Christians one bit!

But there was a problem.

All those Protestants who left? Many of them were business people. And when they left, their businesses went with them. And all their money. In fact, French Protestants helped found the Bank of England and it was even a French Protestant company that printed the Bank of England's bank notes! Some people believe the rise of the English economy during that period can be traced in significant part to the expertise of the French Protestant immigrants fleeing Louis!

So Louis's crazy hatred of French Protestants ended up making his arch enemy, England, much stronger. France lived to regret that!

It wasn't just England that benefited from French intolerance. So did America. In a huge way. Because you know George Washington? One of his ancestors was a French Protestant who first fled to England to escape an early round of persecution, and then came to America to find religious freedom.

If it hadn't been for the persecution of the French Protestants, well, then there would never have been a George Washington. So I suppose all Americans should be thankful in a strange way to the Kings of France for their intolerance of French Protestants!

By the way, French Protestants are called "Huguenots." You may want to check if you have any Huguenot ancestors. They're more common than you might imagine because they fled all over the world.

A Visit to Vaux-le-Vicomte

When I read about Nic's home, I decided I had to go and see it for myself.

When I arrived at Nic's house, which is named Vaux-le-Vicomte, I was stunned. It looks even more astonishingly beautiful in real life than in the pictures. The first thing I saw was a huge, beautiful building. I said to my daughters who were with me, "That really is something special."

But then my oldest daughter said to me, "Dad, that's not the house! Look..." and she pointed to the sign. It said: "Horse Stables." I wasn't looking at Nic's house at all - I was looking at his horse stables? Wow, even Nic's horses lived in a magnificent mansion!

And then I saw the house itself.

I had to stop and stare.

Just imagine it for a minute. There's a long gravel driveway - I mean really long - and at the end is a moat. And in the middle of the moat sits the massive house like its own little island. Well, I just had to see inside, so I walked up the drive, over a beautiful arched stone bridge across the moat and to the front doors located in the center of the large barrel-shaped central wing of the mansion.

At the top of the four-story high building is a beautiful big dome covered in dark grey slate tiles. And at the very tippy top of the dome is a rotunda, with another little dome on top of that and a spike. Two wings of the house branch off to the left and the right, and then jut forward. Each has a high pitched slate roof on them. The entire home is made out of a lovely honey-colored stone.

As soon as we arrived in the house, my kids said, "Let's go right up to the top of that dome!"

I have to admit, I'm not keen on heights. I don't know why. But when I'm up very high, my stomach starts to feel funny, my heart begins to beat to fast, and my legs get wobbly.

And if it were up to me, I'd never go up high!

But when you have kids, they make you do all sorts of things you don't want to!

So, off I went. Up the grand staircase. And then onto smaller stairs. Then into the attic. And pretty soon we were right up in the middle of the dome on rickety old wooden stairs that are hundreds of years old. They creaked with every step. It was terrible!

At the very top we came to a little door. I had to stoop right down to get out. And when I did, I wished I hadn't! Because we were on the smallest of little balconies that wraps around the tiny rotunda at the top of the dome. My kids were laughing and loving it. Me? I was a quaking mess.

Until I stopped looking straight down over the dome and looked out over the gardens.

I suppose the view from the top of the dome is the best way to appreciate those gardens. They really are just perfect - with fountains, ponds, a lake, special flowers and trees. And they just go on, and on, and on, and on.

Old Nic sure knew how to build a house!

Back in the house, it's one wondrous room after another. Our favorite is the room under the dome. It's three stories high, and the walls are made of very high glass doors, with semi-circular windows above them, and then another set of windows above that. The curved domed ceiling is painted like the sky. The door frames and other parts of the walls are all made of white marble. And the floor? It's white and black marble tiles.

If there ever was a magnificent ballroom, this is it! If only poor old Nic got a chance to enjoy it as much as we did... Would you like to see photos of "the most beautiful house in the world?" Visit: www.brownroadbooks.com and click on the Extras button on the right of the top menu - it's worth seeing for yourself!

Monkey Mischief

When I was a boy, I lived on the tropical island of Penang in Malaysia. We didn't have supermarkets, convenience stores or outlet malls. When my mom said we were going to the market, she meant a real outdoor market.

Our local market was called Pulau Tikus, which means "Island of Rats." That's an unfortunate name for a market, don't you think? Whenever we went to the market, my first stop was the pancake man.

The pancake man had a little trolley, and he spread the pancake mix ever so thinly on the round flat metal surface heated by fiery charcoal underneath. Then he added a special mix of ground peanuts and sugar all over the inside of the pancake. Within no time, he'd fold one perfectly brown side of the pancake over so it looked like a big flat taco, and voila, there was the tastiest treat you could ever imagine!

The sweet pancake was so thin, it was always crispy. And the peanut mix in the middle was slightly runny. It's called an apam balik in Malay - which means a pancake turnover. I think it should be called a "tongue teaser tummy pleaser" - it is just so good!

As much as I loved the market, I hated the smell. You see, when you have meat and fish out in the hot air, it really stinks. And the market also had open drains that didn't help. I had to watch very carefully so I didn't fall into them! And the smell coming from them? You really don't want to know!

My family didn't eat meat. But even if we did, I think one visit to that market would have made me a vegetarian as I watched the flies crawling over the smelly raw meat as blood ran down into the drain.

Sorry, that's a bit gross, isn't it!

But there was something that smelled even worse than the meat, fish and drains - a fruit called durian. Durian is the "Stinky Fruit" I wrote about earlier in this book.

At the market, it felt like you could buy almost anything at all from toy cars to spring onions, to… well, on this particular day, monkeys.

~

Even by our market's standards, a monkey for sale was highly unusual.

And suspicious.

You see, some people eat monkeys.

They really shouldn't.

But they do.

And you just had to wonder, who's selling this monkey and what for?

This little brown monkey looked like the most miserable little fellow you've ever seen. It was like he knew bad things were coming his way. And all he wanted to do was to get back to his family in the jungle. He would have leapt off that pole in a second, but a nasty chain was wrapped right around his little neck, and he could barely move without choking.

It was just a heart-breaking scene.

A rather ugly man with a cruel look stood by the monkey waiting for bids.

And that's when my brother Tim exclaimed, "I want that monkey, mom!"

My mom, who had a soft heart, looked at Tim but even soft-hearted mom wasn't going to bring a monkey home.

"I'm sorry Tim, but you already have a dog, three cats, four kittens, five budgies, three fish and five ducks. That's enough pets!"

"But mom, look at this poor little fellow! Don't you feel sorry for him?"

"Of course I do, Tim, but we simply can't add any more animals."

"But mom, look at the chain around his little neck - its so cruel!"

"I know..."

"And look how so utterly sad he looks..."

"I know..."

"And think what they're going to do with the poor little guy..."

Mom looked at the seller and shuddered.

"I know..."

"And, and, and..."

"Tim, I'm telling you, I'd love to help him out, but we're at our absolute limit with animals."

"But mom!"

She motioned for Tim to follow her, and they walked off into the market together. But at every opportunity, Tim talked about that monkey.

They were by the dark-green vegetables, when mom turned around and commanded, "Enough about the monkey, Tim!"

"But mom... his poor little face..."

And that's when my mother had a great idea. She knew Tim was saving every penny for a radio-controlled boat. It was his heart's desire. And not just any boat - *The Sunshine 9000* with its big engine, bright yellow bow, and beautiful sleek design. It was everything he had ever dreamed of. He'd been saving for years. There was nothing he seemed to talk about besides that boat.

So she turned to Tim and said, "Tim, I'm not buying that monkey, and that's final. If you want him, you can buy him with your *own money.*"

Of course, my mom assumed Tim would forget about the monkey. After all, before that moment none of us had ever thought of a pet monkey. Surely he wouldn't give up his dream of *The Sunshine 9000* just for a downcast little monkey. After all, weren't there a million other little monkeys out there in the jungle?

But mom seriously miscalculated.

Tim, looked back, and in an instant shot back, "Yes, take all my money, every penny I've got, and I will buy the monkey!"

Some parents at this point, I suppose, would go back on their word. They'd say something like, "OK, well, let's think about it then." And move on, spending the next few days explaining why owning a monkey is a really bad idea for one reason or another. But that wasn't my mom's style. If she said it, she did it. And she'd given Tim permission to buy it with his own money, and now he was going to. She wasn't about to go back on her word.

The man selling the monkey was quite surprised when Tim came up to bargain with him.

"Why do you want the monkey?" he asked suspiciously.

"He'll be my pet," Tim replied.

"Your pet? Monkeys are not good for pets! They're good for soup!" he said with a crackly laugh.

Tim didn't laugh, he just asked the price in a very business like voice.

After a little back and forth, they settled on a price.

"If he doesn't work out as a pet, you can always bring him back to me," the man laughed again, "as I always like a little monkey in my broth!"

Tim was normally polite, but at this suggestion he just scowled. His precious monkey wasn't going into anyone's soup - that was for sure!

~

When we got home, Tim had to name his new pet. It didn't take long for Tim to come up with Charlie Brown - just like the cartoon character. And the name stuck.

Monkeys are, in truth, quite tricky pets. And Charlie Brown was among the trickiest.

He loved our other pets, but they didn't love him as much. And I can't really blame them.

He liked to jump on the back of our dog, hold onto his fur and ride on his back. Charlie Brown's eyes were alight with joy as he loved every minute of his monkey rodeo.

Our dog's eyes? Not so happy. She looked at us and seemed to say, "Why on earth did you bring this pesky monkey home!"

Charlie Brown also liked our cats. No, he didn't pat them until they purred. Instead, he'd wait until they weren't looking, and then he'd tug on their tails, leap away, and sort of laugh at them.

Our cats did not like Charlie Brown!

He was a menace to the ducks - chasing them around creating so much quacking and confusion, we had to run out and stop him. He didn't care. He loved chasing ducks!

But his favorite activities involved all the interesting things humans have.

One day when we got back from school, we walked into our home. And there in the kitchen was flour spread everywhere, and cups and dishes thrown all over the place.

"What on earth has happened here," exclaimed mom, "it looks like a bomb's exploded!"

She didn't have to guess for long because all over the house were little white flour footprints left by a very guilty looking Charlie Brown.

Mom wasn't happy. Not at all. And that was only the beginning.

When it was my dad's birthday, my mom put a cake on the table. But as soon as she turned her back? Can you guess who jumped onto the table and began helping himself!

Charlie Brown loved my mom's china. He loved my mom's clothes. He loved all her knick-knacks around the house.

Charlie Brown was a lady's worst nightmare!

But all that monkey mischief could be forgiven. It was what happened next that took monkey business to a whole new level.

~

We were sitting at home when there was a very firm knock at the door. My brothers and I looked at each other. "Well, that was a rather loud knock," said Tim, looking surprised. I jumped up to answer, but he called me back, "Maybe it's best for mom to see who's out there..."

When mom answered the door, there was our neighbor. And she looked angry. Really angry.

"Where's that little monkey of yours!" she bellowed, "I want to give him a good hiding!"

"What's all this about?" asked mom.

"It's all about that naughty monkey of yours, that's what!"

"But, but, why?" asked mom as she thought of a thousand possible things Charlie may have done this time!

"This morning I hung all my white sheets out to dry because, as you'll remember, yesterday it was raining."

"Well, yes," replied my mom.

"And as you know, with rain comes mud in our backyard."

"Well, sure."

"Then guess what your little monkey did!"

"I couldn't even begin to guess."

"He got on the washing line, and pulled all my beautiful white sheets off and threw them in the mud. Now why would he do that? What kind of malicious, no good, nasty little monkey brain does he have? Where is he, as he's going to get the full force of my fury!"

"Ok, ok. I'll find him, and I can assure you we'll do our very best to make sure that it never happens again."

"Your very best isn't good enough! That monkey scoundrel will out-smart all of us. He's cunning and conniving!"

Eventually my mom was able to convince our neighbor to leave. Then mom sat down and sighed very loudly.

Tim was looking very worried. He knew Charlie Brown had been an awful lot of trouble. And no one really liked poor Charlie. Well, no one but Tim. Even the dog, cats and ducks weren't fond of him.

"Tim, I've been thinking."

"Uh, ha."

"Well, I'm not really sure Charlie Brown is cut out to be a pet."

"Uh, ha."

"He's really not a house-trained sort of animal, and I'm not sure even how to start to train him. I mean, how do you teach an animal not to do mischief, when he so obviously delights in it. It's hard enough with children, let alone a monkey!"

"Uh, ha."

"And I've been watching Charlie Brown. And every so often he just looks out at the jungle, and I think there's a look in his eyes that says he wants to go back to his real home."

"Oh no. No no no no no! I love Charlie Brown, mom," said Tim with a mix of anger and hurt.

"I know you love him, Tim. But I don't know how much you love him."

"How much? Are you kidding me? I love him with all my heart, that's how much!" Tim replied, surprised.

"Well, if you love him with all your heart, would you let him choose between living in the human world or the monkey world?"

"What do you mean?"

"My hunch is that if Charlie Brown had the choice, he'd prefer the monkey world to living with us. And maybe that's why he's doing all these things that he knows will upset us. I mean, it's one thing to eat a cake, it's another to throw all the washing in the mud. Why would he do that? What does he gain by doing it? It just seems like it's his way of saying, 'Hey, I'm not part of your world - I want to go back to my world.'"

Tim thought for a minute. "But if he went back to his world, mom, that would mean I'd lose him! I don't think my heart could take that!"

"And if you stop him, and he has to live his life away from all he loves, how does that feel?"

Tim sat in silence. Mom had a point. Of course. And it was true that Charlie Brown seemed restless. Something just seemed very wrong.

After what seemed like a very long break, Tim spoke: "Look, I get what you're saying. If I really love Charlie, I'll let him make the choice. But I don't even know how we'd test if he wants to stay with us, or rejoin the monkey world."

"What about this," mom said. "How about we take Charlie Brown to the edge of the jungle. We take some food with us that he likes. We let him out of the box, and then you call to him, showing him the food. If he comes back to you, well that's a pretty good sign he wants to be a pet living with us humans. But if he resists his favorite food and instead runs off into the jungle, that's a good sign that his heart remains up among the vines with the other monkeys."

"Hmmm, that's a sort of sensible plan," replied Tim, hesitantly.

It was hard to sleep that night knowing that the big test would happen the next day. When we woke up, Tim gave strict orders. "You know today we're giving Charlie Brown the jungle test. Everyone has to be super kind to Charlie today. Even if he does another of his monkey tricks - no matter what. Right?"

We all agreed, even mom.

~

When we got home from school, Tim ran over to where Charlie was sitting casually munching on a little banana from the tree in our back garden. Charlie looked lazily over at Tim as if to say, "Hey buddy, where have you been all day?" Tim gently patted Charlie's back, and then scratched him every so carefully behind his little monkey ears.

Tim and Charlie were a perfect match.

As they sat together, Tim talked to Charlie just like a friend. And Charlie? He looked up at Tim every so often, just like he understood perfectly.

"Let's get going," I said to mom, impatient to see how the jungle test was going to play out.

"There's no rush," mom replied, "let's give Tim and Charlie a little bit more time together..."

~

When Tim and Charlie had finished their time together, we prepared to get going. But getting a monkey into a car isn't easy. Particularly when that monkey is Charlie Brown!

As soon as we got in, Charlie leapt into the front and started pushing every button he could find.

Switches went up.

Buttons in.

Charlie flipped the rod and the window wipers started up...

And when Charlie found the horn? Oh boy!

"Get Charlie under control," yelled my mom.

"Sorry mom!" said Tim.

He reached into the front, but Charlie jumped into the back.

Tim flopped back, and Charlie leaped forward!

Back, front, left, right - Charlie was everywhere and nowhere all at once!

Until he made one leap too many. Tim's hands grabbed him in mid-air, and Charlie was put into a big cardboard box. "Don't worry, Charlie," said Tim, "the jungle's only a few minutes away."

We soon pulled over next to the jungle. Tim carefully got a sweet little short banana and a little bit of cake ready. He then opened the car door and placed the box gently on the ground. Then he slowly opened the box lid, reached in, gave Charlie one final gentle pat, and then moved back so Charlie could get out.

It didn't take long.

Charlie jumped out, looked around, and it was almost like the wheels in his brain were turning. He looked at Tim, he looked at the jungle, he looked at Tim, he looked back at the jungle. And he eyed the banana and cake.

And then he leapt back into Tim's arms!

Well, actually that didn't happen. I wish that was the way the story ended, but it isn't. You see Charlie Brown, cautiously at first, and then faster and faster, ran into the jungle. And in no time he was up in the trees swinging around. When another monkey came up to him, that cheeky old Charlie Brown gave the other monkey a good box on the ear. From then on, Charlie was gone from the human world and was back into the monkey world. Forever.

On our way home, Tim was very quiet. He just sat and thought. And thought. And thought. And we all sat quietly, too. Then, as we pulled into the driveway he spoke: "Wow, love really is hard, isn't it?"

～

Tim was right, love is hard! After all, he'd given everything he had to save Charlie Brown. But then, when Charlie Brown was given a choice, well, he didn't choose Tim. Of course, Tim could have caged Charlie Brown, but where would the love in that be? Real love means giving the ones we love the freedom to choose. Because, if we aren't free to choose, then we aren't free to love. Right?

Sometimes people criticize God. They say, if God really exists and if He really loves us, then why does He allow people to do bad things? It's a good question. And there's an equally good answer. God loves us so much that, even after Jesus gave everything He had for us, He gives us the freedom to choose whether to love Him back or not.

Why not force us? Because as soon as you force someone into doing something, you do two things. First, you show that you really don't love them. Second, the person you are forcing to be with you, loses the opportunity to freely love you back.

Love and freedom? They're really two sides of the same coin. You simply can't have love without freedom.

And sometimes that's really hard!

Don't believe me? Ask Tim. He's a research scientist now. He travels the world speaking. He's been on TV and radio. But whenever I mention Charlie Brown, he still has a very soft spot in his heart for the little cheeky monkey. And in truth, so do I.

Of course we went back to the spot where we freed Charlie Brown to look for him. We think we saw him once. He was leading a little troop of monkeys. He stopped and looked at us and there seemed to be that same old Charlie Brown glint in his eyes like, "Hey, what are you guys doing here, and why didn't you bring me any cake!"

~

Recently, I took my girls back to that tropical island where I grew up.

Did I take them to the old open market? Oh yes I did. And guess what? It still stinks as bad as ever. And, as strange as it sounds, that made me happy!

I even tried to get them to eat some durian, but you know what they said to me? "Dad! You'd have to be crazy to eat something that smells that bad!" Well, maybe they're right. Or maybe not. I don't really care. Because I ate lots of it, and loved every minute!

And did we get one of those beautiful peanut pancakes? You bet! And it was so sweet, crunchy and nutty - you really need to try one to believe it.

We did one more thing, too. We drove down to the place where Tim freed Charlie Brown all those years ago. And do you know what we saw? Monkeys. Hundreds of monkeys. Monkeys climbing on trees, monkeys swinging from vines, monkeys running up to us to get peanuts. Monkeys absolutely everywhere. And you know what I wondered? I wondered if any of these cheeky little fellows are Charlie Brown's grandchildren?

I can't say for sure. But there was one who came up awfully close to grab a peanut from me and he had that that very cheeky little Charlie Brown glint in his eyes!

If you want to see pictures of us with monkeys and to hear Charlie Brown's Song visit:

www.brownroadbooks.com and click on the ***Extras*** button on the top menu - you'll get a very good idea of what Charlie Brown looked like :)

Charlie Brown's Song!

Everyone has talents. Some people are good at drawing. Others at singing. Some are good at sports. Others at math. Most of us are good at a few different things, I suppose.

I'm not a particularly good singer. And although I play the guitar, I don't do it especially well. But what I like doing is writing songs. And some of my friends think I do that quite well. I must have great friends!

Anyway, the Charlie Brown story has its own song! Sadly, I can't sing it for you because you're there in reading world, and I'm here in writing world, and I just can't quite squeeze the song over to you. But here are the lyrics and why don't you add your own tune to them? And when you've finished trying your version, you can go to the web address at the end of the story to hear what it sounds like with my tune...

I'm just a monkey
Swinging in a tree
Don't you want to
Swing with me?

I like coconut
Banana too
But most of all
I like people food

What's my name?
Charlie Brown!
Write it down!
Charlie Brown!

What's my name?
Charlie Brown!
Write it down!
Charlie Brown!

What's my name?
Charlie Brown!
Write it down!
Charlie Brown!

My name's Charlie, Charlie, Charlie, Charlie, Charlie, Charlie Brown!

I just looked at the lyrics and they don't seem half as clever as the song sounds when it's sung. I guess that makes sense. It is a song after all, not a poem!

When I tell this story, I have the kids help me sing the song. I sing out "What's my name?" And all the kids yell in unison, "Charlie Brown!" It's a lot of fun. I just told the story at a large school in Maryland - and you know what? The kids did a brilliant job with the "Charlie Browns!" Maybe one day I'll come to your school or your church and we can do it together. I know it'll put a big smile on your face. It always does mine!

If you want to hear Charlie Brown's Song visit:
www.brownroadbooks.com and click on the Extras button

The Final Tale

Do you know the strange thing? I have so many more stories, I suppose they could fill another ten books! And if I don't get too busy with everything else in life, I'll write at least one more. In fact, I've already started the next story book. Do you want a little taste? The first story starts like this -

It was common knowledge in Nunawading, that there was no rival Pathfinder Club in Melbourne quite as repulsive as Warburton. So repulsive, in fact, we called them the "Warby Dorks."

I admit, it wasn't a very nice thing to call them. But then again, they weren't very nice! In fact, they were the worst. Particularly as they always seemed to beat us at everything.

Their marching? Superb!

Their survival skills? Outstanding!

Their campfire lighting? Beat us, again, every time!

Their knot tying? Way ahead of anything we did!

Repelling? Mountain bike riding? Camp cooking? Tent pitching? Flag capturing?

Yep, beat us at all of them.

In fact, I can't ever remember beating them at anything.

Which only went to prove just what a pack of dorks they were. At least that's what we told ourselves as we marched in our wobbly lines, tied knots we could never undo and fell face first in the mud as we tried to catch them running away with our flag.

But all of that changed one day, when our leader announced a big plan.

"There's been a little bad blood between the Nunawading and Warburton Pathfinder clubs," he began in his strong Australian accent.

We all cheered as loud as we could.

"No, no, no. That's not the spirit," he continued his face becoming red. "We want to get on together, right?"

There was a murmuring in the ranks that sounded like anything but agreement.

The counselor looked at us disapprovingly. "We want to go from competition to cooperation, right?"

Another dissenting murmur went up.

"And that's why we've organized a special get together. A sort of peace conference. Time when Nunawading and Warburton can become friends, see?" the counselor pleaded.

My brother Tim looked at me, and smiled, "Yeah, time to become friends, now that sounds like an opportunity for some fun!"

I looked back at Tim and giggled. The Warby Dorks might have beat us at almost everything going. But we were still the champs at one event. Though no one was about to give us a badge of honor for it. Because we were the *kings of the prank*, and I could tell, Tim was cooking up a good prank this time.

"So, I want you to put on your nice face," the counselor continued. And then, he pointed right at Tim, "and that includes you Timothy!" Tim's silly grin didn't inspire confidence in anyone. "You better not mess it up this time!" the counselor said sternly.

Mess it up? A chance to pay the Warby Dorks back for humiliating us at almost everything? Tim wasn't going to mess it up, that was for sure! The Warby Dorks had no idea what was about to hit them! But then again, neither did Tim...

For the rest of this story, and many like them, get ready for James Standish's next book, that is scheduled to come out just in time for summer. To stay in the loop on new books, stories, videos and podcasts, and to get regular updates, send a note to: brownroadbooks@outlook.com

Made in the USA
Middletown, DE
06 March 2017